100 Desserts

TO DIE FOR

✕ TRISH DESEINE ✕

100 Desserts TO DIE FOR

Quick, easy, delicious recipes for the ultimate classics

MURDOCH BOOKS

SYDNEY · LONDON

Introduction

FIRST OF ALL, A DISCLAIMER: the title of this book is meant to be as tongue-in-cheek as Nigella Lawson's cult —but initially misunderstood—cookbook, *How to Be a Domestic Goddess*. Just as Nigella had no intention of wiping out decades of feminist progress by chaining women once again to their stoves, *100 Desserts to Die For* is certainly not an instruction manual for a trip to Dignitas. Its aim is rather to balance out the trend, so widespread these days, of going without dessert.

MARK TWAIN WROTE: 'There are people who strictly deprive themselves of each and every eatable, drinkable, and smokable which has in any way acquired a shady reputation. They pay this price for health. And health is all they get for it. How strange it is. It is like paying out your whole fortune for a cow that has gone dry.'

HAVING SAID THAT, MAYBE THESE DAYS it is cookbooks more than food products that should come with health warnings or traffic light ratings ... If this were the case, this book would be slapped with a sticker saying 'Use with caution', or 'Only handle this book in the presence of a responsible adult'.

WHILE IT IS TRUE that a diet made up entirely of these impossibly sweet and rich desserts would in effect lead you towards an early grave, you shouldn't feel obliged to gorge yourself on them, all caution thrown to the wind, until your heart, arteries, liver and tastebuds throw in the towel and shut up shop, encrusted with sugar.

I ENTRUST THESE RECIPES TO YOU in the certainty that, as responsible adults, you will make them enthusiastically at sensible intervals—say, once a week? Keeping this in mind, I have tried to be as exhaustive as possible in my selection of recipes, which I have organised according to my most frequently recurring cravings when I think 'dessert'. Sometimes—let's say most of the time!—it's chocolate I want, although often I feel like something sweet and creamy. In summer and autumn I lean towards fruit and ice creams, and for Sunday meals and family gatherings, I often turn to French classics and soft cakes. There are several recipes that use—celebrate, I should say!—some slightly 'trashy' mass-produced ingredients, but most of the time my desserts are made from the most traditional and accessible ingredients you can find.

FAR FROM BEING WEEPY, morbid or excessive, *100 Desserts to Die For* is a great celebration of the joy of (still, and for as long as possible) being alive. After all, dying is the most universal of activities, isn't it? It is something we will all do—in the short, medium or long term, of course—but why not do it well? We can try to convince ourselves we have some sort of control over how we will go, but the truth is it is more or less like playing a giant lottery.

SO IF, LIKE ME, sweet things are at the top of your list of little pleasures you allow yourself from time to time while approaching your inevitable demise, I hope this book will give you a wide range of options to choose from between now and judgement day.

I WILL LEAVE YOU TO YOUR KITCHEN and your life (for now!) with this wise quote from the French humorist Pierre Desproges: 'Let us live happily while we're waiting for death!'

Trish Deseine

I • CLASSICS / *Classiques*

II • CHOCOLATE / *Chocolat*

III • CREAMY / *Crémeux*

IV • SOFT / *Moelleux*

16

6

· CLASSICS ·

Classiques

59

✕ BANOFFEE PIE ✕

There's no need to go to the trouble of making your own caramel for this recipe, as your local supermarket is no doubt loaded with jars of salted butter caramel or dulce de leche. You can't cut corners with the digestive biscuits, however.

300 g (10½ oz) digestive biscuits (sweet wholemeal biscuits)

100 g (3½ oz) lightly salted butter, melted

200 g (7 oz) salted butter caramel or dulce de leche (see page 129)

3 bananas, fairly ripe

300 ml (10½ fl oz) thin (pouring/whipping) cream, well chilled

2 tablespoons mascarpone cheese

50 g (1¾ oz) icing (confectioners') sugar (optional)

Grated dark chocolate, to decorate

CRUSH THE BISCUITS INTO CRUMBS. Combine them with the melted butter and spread the mixture over the base of a round 20–22 cm (8–8½ inch) tart tin. Press down well, then place the base in the fridge for a few minutes to firm it up.

NEXT, SPREAD THE CARAMEL OR DULCE DE LECHE OVER THE PIE BASE. You can heat it up a little beforehand to make it easier to spread.

SLICE THE BANANAS AND ARRANGE THE SLICES ON TOP OF THE CARAMEL.

WHIP THE CREAM AND MASCARPONE TOGETHER WITH AN ELECTRIC BEATER UNTIL LIGHT, ADDING THE ICING SUGAR IF NEEDED. Spread this mixture over the banana slices.

DECORATE WITH GRATED CHOCOLATE AND SERVE IMMEDIATELY, OR KEEP THE BANOFFEE PIE IN THE FRIDGE UNTIL SERVING TIME.

× PAVLOVA ×

A cushion of cream on a cloud of sugar with crunchy edges. This is a dream dessert – my favourite!

4 egg whites, at room temperature
220 g (7¾ oz/1 cup) caster (superfine) sugar
1 teaspoon vinegar or lemon juice
1 tablespoon cornflour (cornstarch)
½ teaspoon natural vanilla extract
300 ml (10½ fl oz) thin (pouring/whipping) cream, well chilled
2 heaped tablespoons mascarpone cheese
300 g (10½ oz) mixed raspberries and halved strawberries

PREHEAT THE OVEN TO 170°C (325°F/GAS 3). Beat the egg whites to soft peaks in a mixing bowl using an electric beater, then add the sugar in several stages, beating well after each addition, until you have a meringue that is smooth, firm and glossy. Allow about 4–5 minutes for this. Test the texture of the meringue by rubbing a little bit between your fingers; you should not be able to feel any grains of sugar. If it is still grainy, beat for a few moments more. The sugar needs to be completely dissolved, otherwise it can turn into a syrup that oozes out of the pavlova during cooking.

COMBINE THE VINEGAR OR LEMON JUICE WITH THE CORNFLOUR AND VANILLA EXTRACT IN A BOWL. Sprinkle this mixture over the meringue, then gently mix in.

LINE A BAKING TRAY WITH BAKING PAPER. Using a flexible spatula, pile the meringue on the tray in a round heap about 15 cm (6 inches) across, then flatten it slightly in the middle, smoothing the sides a little but without losing too much height.

PLACE IN THE OVEN AND IMMEDIATELY LOWER THE TEMPERATURE TO 120°C (235°F/GAS ½) AND COOK FOR 1 HOUR. Next, turn off the oven and let the pavlova dry out completely with the oven door half open.

WHIP THE CREAM AND MASCARPONE TOGETHER WITH AN ELECTRIC BEATER UNTIL LIGHT. Spread this cream over the pavlova and decorate with fresh raspberries and strawberries before serving.

✕ CHOCOLATE CAFÉ ✕
Liégeois

This ice cream sundae was originally made by pouring cold sweetened coffee over vanilla ice cream, then serving the whole thing with whipped cream. Chocolate was gradually introduced into the mix, giving the dessert a thicker sauce. Personally I am fond of a hybrid version of café Liégeois that combines chocolate, coffee and a good ice cream, which I hope you'll find a change from the soulless and formulaic versions served in many French brasseries.

6 scoops good quality
vanilla ice cream

For the sauce:

200 g (7 oz) dark chocolate,
roughly chopped
200 ml (7 fl oz) thin (pouring/
whipping) cream
2 teaspoons very strong
espresso coffee
50 g (1¾ oz) lightly salted butter

For the whipped cream:

200 ml (7 fl oz) thin (pouring/
whipping) cream, well chilled
2 tablespoons mascarpone cheese
1 tablespoon icing (confectioners')
sugar

MAKE THE SAUCE BY HEATING TOGETHER THE CHOCOLATE, CREAM, COFFEE AND BUTTER IN A SAUCEPAN, OR IN A MIXING BOWL PLACED OVER A SAUCEPAN OF GENTLY SIMMERING WATER. Stir until the sauce is quite smooth and let it cool.

MAKE THE WHIPPED CREAM. Whip the cream with an electric beater until light, incorporating the mascarpone and icing sugar.

ASSEMBLE THE SUNDAES BY PLACING A SCOOP OF ICE CREAM IN EACH DESSERT DISH. Pour over the chocolate-coffee sauce and finish with a little whipped cream. Add some crushed nuts if you like, and serve.

✕ MILK CHOCOLATE AND SALTED ✕
butter caramel mousse

SERVES 6 / 10 MINS PREPARATION TIME /
5 HRS REFRIGERATION TIME

This is a classic that seems to please the majority of people. If you can, use a good quality milk chocolate with a cocoa content of more than 35%.

100 g (3½ oz) caster (superfine) sugar	50 g (1¾ oz) lightly salted butter
200 ml (7 fl oz) thin (pouring/whipping) cream	200 g (7 oz) milk chocolate
	3 eggs

MAKE A CARAMEL. Place the sugar and 1 tablespoon of water in a saucepan. Bring to the boil, then simmer until the syrup caramelises.

HEAT THE CREAM IN ANOTHER SAUCEPAN. Take the caramel off the heat and add the butter and hot cream. Stir well to dissolve any clumps of sugar that form.

COOL THE CARAMEL SLIGHTLY BEFORE ADDING THE CHOCOLATE, BROKEN UP INTO PIECES. Stir to melt the chocolate.

ONCE THE MIXTURE HAS COMPLETELY COOLED, SEPARATE THE EGGS AND BEAT THE WHITES TO SOFT PEAKS USING AN ELECTRIC BEATER.

LIGHTLY BEAT THE YOLKS AND ADD THEM TO THE CHOCOLATE CREAM. Next, fold the egg whites very gently into the chocolate cream, lifting and turning the chocolate cream with a flexible spatula.

DIVIDE THE MOUSSE BETWEEN GLASSES, SMALL DESSERT BOWLS OR RAMEKINS, THEN LET THEM SET IN THE FRIDGE FOR AT LEAST 4-5 HOURS BEFORE SERVING.

× L'AMI JEAN'S ×
rice pudding with caramel

SERVES 6 / 10 MINS PREPARATION TIME / 2 HRS COOKING TIME

A veritable ode to indulgence, this dish (inspired by one from a restaurant in Paris' 7th arrondissement) is a dessert buffet all by itself. The amazingly creamy rice is served with whipped cream and caramelised pecans. The recipe is long, but the result is truly worth it. If you serve this rice pudding when friends come to dinner, don't plan on a starter or cheese course!

For the rice pudding:

200 g (7 oz) arborio rice
1 litre (35 fl oz/4 cups) full-cream (whole) milk
200 g (7 oz) caster (superfine) sugar
200 ml (7 fl oz) crème anglaise (see recipe next page, leaving out the chocolate)
200 ml (7 fl oz) thin (pouring/whipping) cream, well chilled
6 tablespoons salted butter caramel (see recipe previous page)

For the caramelised pecans:

100 g (3½ oz/1 cup) pecans
125 g (4½ oz) caster (superfine) sugar

PLACE THE RICE IN A LARGE SAUCEPAN WITH THE MILK. Bring to the boil and simmer on a very low heat for about 2 hours, stirring regularly. Add more milk if the rice starts to dry out during cooking, as it should be meltingly soft.

TURN OFF THE HEAT AND ADD THE SUGAR, THEN STIR UNTIL COMPLETELY DISSOLVED. Let the rice cool, then mix in the crème anglaise. Place the mixture in the fridge until completely cool.

USING AN ELECTRIC BEATER, WHIP THE CREAM UNTIL LIGHT, THEN COMBINE WITH THE RICE MIXTURE. SET A LITTLE WHIPPED CREAM ASIDE FOR SERVING.

CARAMELISE THE PECANS IN A FRYING PAN WITH THE SUGAR. Heat the salted butter caramel in a saucepan a little to soften, then serve it with the rice, the rest of the whipped cream and the caramelised pecans.

✕ FLOATING ISLANDS ✕

SERVES 4 / 30 MINS PREPARATION TIME / 30 MINS COOKING TIME

Served with a plain or chocolate crème anglaise, floating islands are very easy to make and deliciously retro.

For the crème anglaise:

150 ml (5 fl oz) fresh full-cream (whole) milk

150 ml (5 fl oz) thin (pouring/whipping) cream

1 vanilla bean

4 egg yolks

50 g (1¾ oz) caster (superfine) sugar

50 g (1¾ oz) dark chocolate, roughly chopped (optional)

50 g (1¾ oz/½ cup) flaked almonds, toasted

For the meringues:

4 egg whites

1 litre (35 fl oz/4 cups) full-cream (whole) milk

For the caramel:

50 g (1¾ oz) caster (superfine) sugar

MAKE THE CRÈME ANGLAISE. Bring the milk and cream to the boil in a saucepan with the vanilla bean, split in two lengthways.

MEANWHILE, BEAT THE EGG YOLKS WITH THE SUGAR IN A MIXING BOWL UNTIL THE MIXTURE IS PALE AND HAS DOUBLED IN VOLUME. Pour the milk and cream mixture over the beaten egg yolks and stir. Return this mixture to the saucepan and place on a very gentle heat. Stir constantly with a wooden spoon until the custard thickens. Watch out, it mustn't cook!

ONCE THE CUSTARD IS THICK ENOUGH TO COAT THE BACK OF THE WOODEN SPOON, TAKE IT OFF THE HEAT AND POUR IMMEDIATELY INTO A LARGE COLD MIXING BOWL TO STOP IT COOKING ANY FURTHER. If you decide to make the chocolate version, melt the chocolate in the crème anglaise at this stage and mix together well.

COOL THE CRÈME ANGLAISE WITHOUT REMOVING THE VANILLA BEAN, THEN SET IT ASIDE IN THE FRIDGE SO IT IS WELL CHILLED BEFORE SERVING.

FOR THE MERINGUES, BEAT THE EGG WHITES TO STIFF PEAKS WITH AN ELECTRIC BEATER. Heat the milk in a large saucepan until just simmering, then divide the beaten egg whites into four portions and poach them for a few minutes in the milk. You can also cook them for 15 seconds in a dish in the microwave.

MAKE A CARAMEL BY MELTING AND COLOURING THE SUGAR IN A SAUCEPAN (OR USE SOME READY-MADE CARAMEL). Divide the crème anglaise between dessert bowls, place the poached meringues on top and decorate with threads of caramel and toasted flaked almonds before serving.

COFFEE, CHOCOLATE AND HAZELNUT
dacquoise

SERVES 10 / 1 HR PREPARATION TIME / 1 HR 15 MINS COOKING TIME

An impressive dessert, made up of layers of meringue, hazelnut praline, chocolate ganache and coffee cream. Delectable!

For the meringue:

250 g (9 oz) blanched hazelnuts

300 g (10½ oz) caster (superfine) sugar

25 g (1 oz) cornflour (cornstarch)

6 egg whites

1 pinch salt

For the chocolate ganache:

150 g (5½ oz) dark chocolate

125 g (4½ oz) thin (pouring/whipping) cream

For the coffee cream:

4 egg yolks

50 g (1¾ oz) cornflour (cornstarch)

125 g (4½ oz) caster (superfine) sugar

600 ml (21 fl oz) full-cream (whole) milk

2 tablespoons very strong espresso coffee

200 ml (7 fl oz) thin (pouring/whipping) cream, well chilled

For the hazelnut praline:

150 g (5½ oz/⅔ cup) caster (superfine) sugar

150 g (5½ oz) blanched, toasted hazelnuts

MAKE THE MERINGUE. PREHEAT THE OVEN TO 180°C (350°F/GAS 4). Grind the hazelnuts in a food processor, not too finely. Spread the ground hazelnuts on a baking tray and toast in the oven for 10-12 minutes, stirring once or twice. Let them cool. Combine the ground hazelnuts with 100 g (3½ oz) of the sugar and the cornstarch.

LOWER THE TEMPERATURE OF THE OVEN TO 150°C (300°F/GAS 2). Beat the egg whites with the salt to soft peaks in a mixing bowl, then add the rest of the sugar and beat for 2 minutes until you have a firm and glossy meringue. Fold in the hazelnut mixture using a large spoon.

MAKE 3 DISCS OF MERINGUE, EACH ABOUT 20 CM (8 INCHES) IN DIAMETER, ON SOME BAKING PAPER. You can use a piping bag to do this if you like. Bake the meringues for 1 hour, rotating the baking trays regularly so the meringues cook evenly. Turn off the oven and let the meringues cool with the oven door ajar.

MAKE THE GANACHE. Break the chocolate into pieces in a mixing bowl. Heat the cream in a saucepan and pour it over the chocolate. Let it stand for 1 minute, then stir to melt the chocolate. Let the mixture cool.

MAKE THE COFFEE CREAM. Whisk the egg yolks with the cornflour and sugar until they are pale and have doubled in volume.

BRING THE MILK TO THE BOIL IN A SAUCEPAN. Pour it over the egg yolks and add the coffee, whisking at the same time. Return the mixture to the saucepan and simmer for 2 minutes on a very gentle heat, stirring at the same time. The custard will thicken. Take it off the heat and cover with plastic wrap in contact with the surface of the custard, and let it cool.

WHIP THE CREAM WITH AN ELECTRIC BEATER UNTIL LIGHT, THEN GRADUALLY FOLD IT INTO THE COFFEE CUSTARD.

MAKE THE PRALINE. Melt the sugar in a saucepan to make a caramel. Roughly chop the hazelnuts and spread them over some baking paper or a silicone mat. Pour over the caramel. Let the praline harden and set aside to use for decoration.

TO ASSEMBLE THE DACQUOISE, SPREAD A LAYER OF CHOCOLATE GANACHE ON THE MERINGUES, FOLLOWED BY A LAYER OF THE COFFEE CREAM. Finish with a disc of meringue and decorate with the praline, broken into pieces.

✕ VACHERIN ✕

SERVES 8 / 30 MINS PREPARATION TIME / 1 HR COOKING TIME / 2 HRS RESTING TIME / 1 NIGHT FREEZING TIME

After the 'I did it all myself' of the dacquoise (page 29), give yourself a bit of a rest with this vacherin. You can even skip making the meringue and buy one ready-made for the meringue layer of your ice-cream cake.

3 egg whites
200 g (7 oz) caster (superfine) sugar
500 g (1 lb 2 oz) vanilla ice cream
500 g (1 lb 2 oz) raspberry or strawberry sorbet
250 ml (9 fl oz/1 cup) thin (pouring/whipping) cream, well chilled
2 tablespoons mascarpone cheese
50 g (1¾ oz) icing (confectioners') sugar
1 teaspoon natural vanilla extract

PREHEAT THE OVEN TO 150°C (300°F/GAS 2). Beat the egg whites and 50 g (1¾ oz) of the sugar to soft peaks in a mixing bowl using an electric beater, then add the rest of the sugar, little by little, until the meringue is firm and glossy.

ON A BAKING TRAY LINED WITH BAKING PAPER OR A SILICONE MAT, SPREAD OUT THE MERINGUE TO MAKE 2 DISCS ABOUT 20 CM (8 INCHES) IN DIAMETER. You can make the discs out of spirals of meringue using a piping bag. Immediately lower the temperature of the oven to 100°C (200°F/Gas ½) and bake for 1 hour. Turn off the oven and let the meringues cool for 2 hours with the oven door ajar.

PLACE ONE OF THE MERINGUE DISCS IN A HIGH-SIDED 20 CM (8 INCH) ROUND SPRING-FORM CAKE TIN. Trim the edges if you need to so the disc fits inside the tin.

SPREAD A LAYER OF VANILLA ICE CREAM ON THE FIRST MERINGUE DISC, THEN A LAYER OF RASPBERRY OR STRAWBERRY SORBET. Smooth the surface before placing the second disc of meringue on top, pressing down very lightly.

USING AN ELECTRIC BEATER, WHIP THE CREAM WITH THE MASCARPONE, ICING SUGAR AND VANILLA EXTRACT UNTIL LIGHT. Top the vacherin with the whipped cream. Place the vacherin in the freezer until the cream has set.

TO UNMOULD THE VACHERIN, TAKE IT OUT OF THE FREEZER 20 MINUTES BEFORE SERVING AND WARM THE SURFACE OF THE TIN WITH YOUR HANDS. Serve the vacherin with fresh fruit, whipped cream and a raspberry or strawberry coulis on the side.

✕ MONT BLANC BITES ✕

MAKES ABOUT 12 BITES / 15 MINS PREPARATION TIME / 35 MINS COOKING TIME / 1 HR RESTING TIME

This version of Mont Blanc is a long way from the original version, like the one served at the Angelina tea salon in Paris with its little mountain of crème de marrons spaghetti on a nest of meringue. Here, I have left the crème de marrons in its natural state and I serve it with whipped cream AND crème fraîche for a hint of tartness in the middle of all the sugar.

For the meringue:	For the whipped cream:
3 egg whites	200 ml (7 fl oz) thin (pouring/ whipping) cream, well chilled
120 g (4¼ oz) caster (superfine) sugar	200 g (7 oz) crème fraîche
1 teaspoon natural vanilla extract	About 6 tablespoons crème de marrons (sweet chestnut spread)

PREHEAT THE OVEN TO 150°C (300°F/GAS 2). Line a baking tray with baking paper or a silicone mat.

MAKE THE MERINGUE. Beat the egg whites to form peaks, not too stiff, in a mixing bowl with an electric beater. Add the sugar, little by little, beating well between each addition. Add the vanilla extract and mix together well. The meringue needs to be quite glossy and firm, and the sugar completely dissolved. To test the texture of the meringue, rub a little bit of mixture between your fingers; you shouldn't be able to feel the grains of sugar.

USING A PIPING BAG OR SIMPLY A TEASPOON, PLACE SMALL MOUNDS OF MERINGUE ON THE BAKING TRAY. Bake the meringues for 35 minutes until they are crunchy and slightly golden. Turn off the oven and let the meringues dry out and cool completely for about 1 hour.

WHIP THE CREAM UNTIL LIGHT USING AN ELECTRIC BEATER. Place 1 teaspoon of whipped cream and crème fraîche on each meringue, before finishing with a little crème de marrons.

× TARTE TATIN ×
with Calvados crème fraîche

SERVES 6 / 10 MINS PREPARATION TIME / 30 MINS COOKING TIME

A must-have! This dessert is very easy to make, even easier if you use a cast-iron pan that can go from the stove top to the oven.

For the tart:

3 tart cooking apples
100 g (3½ oz) caster (superfine) sugar
75 g (2½ oz) lightly salted butter
1 round ready-to-use puff pastry

For the Calvados crème fraîche:

200 g (7 oz) crème fraîche
2 tablespoons icing (confectioners') sugar
2 tablespoons Calvados

PREHEAT THE OVEN TO 180°C (350°F/GAS 4). Peel the apples, cut them into segments and remove the seeds.

HEAT THE CASTER SUGAR WITH 2 TABLESPOONS OF WATER IN A TARTE TATIN DISH OR AN OVENPROOF CAST-IRON FRYING PAN. Let it bubble until it caramelises, tilting the pan to distribute it evenly. Remove the dish or frying pan from the heat and add the butter.

STIR THE CARAMEL VERY GENTLY BEFORE LAYING THE APPLE SEGMENTS ON TOP. Cook for 3-4 minutes on a very gentle heat. Turn the apple segments over once (arranging them in a pretty rosette pattern if you like).

COVER THE APPLES WITH THE PUFF PASTRY, TUCKING THE EDGES INTO THE SIDE OF THE DISH OR FRYING PAN. Bake for about 25 minutes. The top of the pastry should be golden brown.

MEANWHILE, COMBINE THE CRÈME FRAÎCHE WITH THE ICING SUGAR AND CALVADOS IN A BOWL.

TAKE THE TART OUT OF THE OVEN AND LET IT COOL FOR 3 MINUTES BEFORE TURNING IT OUT INTO A LARGE, DEEP DISH (TO CATCH ALL THE CARAMEL!). Serve with the calvados crème fraîche.

× DARK CHOCOLATE TART ×

SERVES 8-10 / 20 MINS PREPARATION TIME /
20 MINS COOKING TIME / 3 HRS RESTING TIME

*The most sensual and consensual, in my
opinion, of the classic tarts ...*

1 round ready-to-use shortcrust pastry	3 egg yolks
300 g (10½ oz) dark chocolate	40 g (1½ oz) unsalted butter
200 g (7 oz) thin (pouring/whipping) cream	

PREHEAT THE OVEN TO 200°C (400°F/GAS 6), THEN BLIND BAKE THE PASTRY. To do this, lay the pastry in a tart tin or loaf (bar) tin and line it with baking paper. Cover with pastry weights (ceramic beads or dry beans). Bake the tart case for 20 minutes, until it is nice and golden. Let it cool completely after taking it out of the oven.

BREAK THE CHOCOLATE INTO PIECES IN A MIXING BOWL. Heat the cream in a saucepan, then pour it over the chocolate. Mix well to melt the chocolate. Add the eggs and butter, mixing in well.

POUR THE CHOCOLATE FILLING INTO THE TART CASE, THEN LET IT COOL FOR ABOUT 3 HOURS BEFORE SERVING, TO SET THE CHOCOLATE.

✕ TARTE AU CITRON ✕

SERVES 8 / 1 HR PREPARATION TIME / 1 HR REFRIGERATION TIME / 30 MINS FREEZING TIME / 40 MINS COOKING TIME

Add this great classic to your repertoire of favourite desserts! Although a little technical, this tart is quite easy to master, especially as it is inspired by the foolproof recipe of Delia Smith, the high priestess of British cooking.

For the pastry:

175 g (6 oz) plain (all-purpose) flour

1 pinch salt

75 g (2½ oz) unsalted butter, softened

50 g (1¾ oz) icing (confectioners') sugar

1 egg yolk, lightly beaten with 1 tablespoon of water

For the lemon filling:

5 egg yolks

150 g (5½ oz) caster (superfine) sugar

Grated zest and juice of 5 lemons

175 ml (5½ fl oz) thin (pouring/whipping) cream

2 tablespoons mascarpone cheese

MAKE THE PASTRY. Place the flour and salt into a large mixing bowl with the butter and work them together with your fingertips until you have a mixture that looks like breadcrumbs. Sift the icing sugar and combine it with this mixture, then add the beaten egg yolk.

SHAPE INTO A BALL OF DOUGH AND WRAP IT IN PLASTIC WRAP. Let it rest for 1 hour in the fridge.

MEANWHILE, MAKE THE LEMON FILLING. Lightly beat the egg yolks with the sugar in a mixing bowl. Don't over-whisk, as the mixture might thicken. Add the lemon zest and juice, then add the cream and mascarpone. Whisk well.

ROLL OUT THE PASTRY AND USE IT TO LINE A ROUND TART TIN WITH A DIAMETER OF 22 CM (8½ INCHES) AND A DEPTH OF 4 CM (1½ INCHES). Prick the base with a fork and let it rest in the freezer for 30 minutes. Preheat the oven to 190°C (375°F/Gas 5). Cover the base with baking paper and place pastry weights on top (ceramic beads or dry beans). Blind bake the tart case for 20 minutes. Take the tin out of the oven and lower the temperature to 150°C (300°F/Gas 2).

FILL THE TART CASE WITH THE LEMON FILLING, THEN BAKE FOR ABOUT 30 MINUTES, UNTIL THE CREAM LOOKS LIKE IT HAS JUST SET. Take the tart out of the oven and let it cool for 20 minutes, if you'd like to serve it warm. Otherwise, place it in the fridge so it cools down completely. You can serve it dusted with icing sugar with whipped cream alongside.

× PEAR AND ALMOND ×
tart

SERVES 8 / 40 MINS PREPARATION TIME / 1 HR REFRIGERATION TIME / 30 MINS RESTING TIME / 1 HR COOKING TIME

It is the almond filling that gives this elegant tart all of its aroma. If you prefer, you can replace the pears with cherries.

For the pastry:

175 g (6 oz) plain (all-purpose) flour

1 pinch salt

75 g (2½ oz) unsalted butter, softened

50 g (1¾ oz) icing (confectioners') sugar

1 egg yolk, lightly beaten with 1 tablespoon of water

For the filling:

175 g (6 oz/1¾ cups) almond meal

1 teaspoon sugar

1 teaspoon plain (all-purpose) flour

90 g (3¼ oz) unsalted butter, softened

1 whole egg and 1 egg white

1 teaspoon natural almond essence

1 tablespoon kirsch

6 tinned poached pears

MAKE THE PASTRY. Place the flour and salt into a large mixing bowl with the butter and work them together with your fingertips until the mixture resembles breadcrumbs. Sift the icing sugar and combine with this mixture, then add the beaten egg yolk.

SHAPE INTO A BALL OF DOUGH AND WRAP IN PLASTIC WRAP. Let it rest in the fridge for 1 hour.

ROLL OUT THE PASTRY AND USE IT TO LINE A 22 CM (8½ INCH) ROUND TART TIN. Prick it with a fork and let it rest in the freezer for 30 minutes. Preheat the oven to 190°C (375°F/Gas 5). Cover the pastry case with baking paper and place pastry weights on top (ceramic beads or dry beans). Blind bake the tart case for 20 minutes.

MAKE THE FILLING. Combine the almond meal with the sugar and flour in a mixing bowl. Next, mix in the butter, the whole egg and egg white, the almond essence and kirsch, beating well after each addition. Fill the pastry case with this mixture.

CUT THE PEARS INTO 2 CM (¾ INCH) SLICES AND ARRANGE THEM IN A ROSETTE PATTERN ON TOP OF THE ALMOND CREAM. Lightly press them into the cream.

BAKE THE TART FOR ABOUT 40 MINUTES UNTIL IT IS PUFFED UP AND GOLDEN. Take it out of the oven and let it cool slightly before serving, if you'd like to serve it warm. Otherwise let it cool completely in the fridge.

✕ CHERRY CLAFOUTIS ✕

SERVES 8 / 5 MINS PREPARATION TIME / 35 MINS COOKING TIME

A baked crêpe batter filled with cherries, what's not to like about this quick dessert that smells of sunny days?

60 g (2¼ oz) plain (all-purpose) flour

3 eggs

60 g (2¼ oz) caster (superfine) sugar

300 ml (10½ fl oz) fresh full-cream (whole) milk

½ teaspoon natural vanilla extract

300 g (10½ oz) cherries (pitted if you have the energy)

PREHEAT THE OVEN TO 180°C (350°F/GAS 4). Butter a gratin dish.

PLACE ALL OF THE INGREDIENTS (EXCEPT THE CHERRIES) IN A MIXING BOWL AND MIX THEM TOGETHER WITH AN ELECTRIC BEATER.

ARRANGE THE CHERRIES IN THE GRATIN DISH AND POUR OVER THE BATTER. Scatter over a little sugar and bake for 30–35 minutes, until the surface of the clafoutis is puffed up and golden brown and the cherries start to release their juices.

TAKE THE CLAFOUTIS OUT OF THE OVEN AND SERVE HOT OR JUST WARM.

✕ FONTAINEBLEAU ✕

SERVES 4 / 20 MINS PREPARATION TIME /
2 HRS REFRIGERATION TIME

The 'true' recipe for Fontainebleau, as I have given it to you here, is a little fiddly. If you don't have the time or inclination, you can skip the draining stage and serve a 'false' Fontainebleau after whipping the cream with the faisselle cheese.

300 g (10½ oz) faisselle (soft curd) cheese (or 50/50 thick yoghurt and cottage cheese)

1 tablespoon orange flower water

300 g (10½ oz) thin (pouring/whipping) cream, well chilled

50 g (1¾ oz) vanilla sugar

200 g (7 oz (1⅓ cups) strawberries, sliced

50 g (1¾ oz) honey

Special equipment:

Muslin (cheesecloth)

BEAT THE FAISSELLE CHEESE WITH THE ORANGE FLOWER WATER USING AN ELECTRIC BEATER. Whip the cream and vanilla sugar together until light. Fold it into the faisselle mixture.

LINE A STRAINER WITH MUSLIN (CHEESECLOTH) AND PLACE IT OVER A MIXING BOWL. Pour the whipped cream-faisselle mixture into the strainer. Let it drain for at least 2 hours in the fridge, so it loses some of its liquid.

YOU CAN ALSO MAKE 4 SMALL FONTAINEBLEAUS BY CAREFULLY PLACING 4 PIECES OF MUSLIN IN THE STRAINER.

SERVE THE FONTAINEBLEAU WITH THE SLICED STRAWBERRIES AND THE HONEY ON THE SIDE.

✕ CLASSIC CRÈME ✕
caramel

MAKES 6 x 150 ML (5 FL OZ) RAMEKINS / 30 MINS PREPARATION TIME /
30 MINS COOKING TIME / 1 NIGHT RESTING TIME

A great classic in any self-respecting dessert repertoire.

For the caramel:

175 g (6 oz) caster (superfine) sugar

For the custard:

4 eggs
1 teaspoon natural vanilla extract
25 g (1 oz) caster (superfine) sugar
300 ml (10½ fl oz) thin (pouring/whipping) cream
300 ml (10½ fl oz) full-cream (whole) milk

GREASE THE RAMEKINS WITH A LITTLE BUTTER. Place them in the oven and preheat to 150°C (300°F/Gas 2) (the ramekins need to be very hot to take the caramel).

MAKE THE CARAMEL. Place the sugar in a saucepan with 100 ml (3½ fl oz) of water. Heat to dissolve the sugar, then let it bubble until a caramel forms and turns a lovely mahogany colour. Pour the caramel into the hot ramekins.

LET THE CARAMEL COOL AND SET AT ROOM TEMPERATURE (NOT IN THE FRIDGE, TO AVOID THERMAL SHOCKS).

MEANWHILE, MAKE THE CUSTARD. Beat the eggs with the vanilla extract and caster sugar in a mixing bowl.

BRING THE CREAM AND MILK TO THE BOIL IN A SAUCEPAN, THEN POUR THEM THROUGH A STRAINER OVER THE EGGS, WHISKING AT THE SAME TIME. Once the custard is nice and smooth, pour it into the ramekins on top of the caramel.

PLACE THE RAMEKINS IN A BAKING TIN OR DISH AND FILL IT WITH WATER TO REACH HALF WAY UP THE SIDE OF THE RAMEKINS. Bake for 20–30 minutes in this bain-marie, until the custard is just set. Don't allow bubbles to form in the custard.

TAKE THE BAKING DISH OUT OF THE OVEN AND LET THE CRÈMES COOL BEFORE PLACING THEM IN THE FRIDGE OVERNIGHT, SO THE CUSTARD ABSORBS THE CARAMEL.

THE NEXT DAY, RUN A KNIFE AROUND THE EDGE OF THE RAMEKINS TO LOOSEN THE CRÈMES. Turn them out onto deep plates and serve them with whipped cream if you like.

$\times$ FINANCIERS $\times$

MAKES 12 FINANCIERS / 20 MINS PREPARATION TIME / 12 MINS COOKING TIME

Little cakes with the delicious flavour of butter ... An essential recipe that's a must to master.

90 g (3¼ oz) unsalted butter

70 g (2½ oz/⅔ cup) almond meal

85 g (3 oz/⅔ cup) icing (confectioners') sugar

30 g (1 oz) plain (all-purpose) flour

3 egg whites

1 pinch salt

½ teaspoon natural vanilla extract

Special equipment:

12-hole financier tin

PREHEAT THE OVEN TO 200°C (400°F/GAS 6). Butter and flour the financier tin. Gently melt the butter in a saucepan or a microwave.

COMBINE THE ALMOND MEAL, ICING SUGAR AND FLOUR IN A MIXING BOWL. In another mixing bowl, beat the egg whites with the salt to soft peaks using an electric beater.

POUR THE MELTED BUTTER AND VANILLA EXTRACT INTO THE MIXING BOWL WITH THE FLOUR AND ALMOND MEAL, THEN COMBINE. Next, gently fold in the beaten egg whites, lifting and turning the mixture with a flexible spatula.

FILL EACH HOLE OF THE FINANCIER TIN HALF WAY UP WITH THE BATTER, THEN BAKE FOR 10-12 MINUTES UNTIL THE TOPS OF THE FINANCIERS ARE GOLDEN BROWN AND SPRING BACK WHEN YOU PRESS THEM WITH A FINGER.

TAKE THE FINANCIERS OUT OF THE OVEN AND LET THEM COOL FOR 5 MINUTES IN THE TIN BEFORE UNMOULDING THEM. Let them cool completely on a rack before serving.

✕ MADELEINES ✕

After financiers, this is the second in the duo of little French cake recipes to learn by heart.

2 eggs

100 g (3½ oz) caster (superfine) sugar

100 g (3½ oz/⅔ cup) plain (all-purpose) flour

Grated zest and juice of 1 lemon

1 teaspoon baking powder

100 g (3½ oz) lightly salted butter, melted

Special equipment:

Madeleine tins

PREHEAT THE OVEN TO 200°C (400°F/GAS 6). Brush the moulds of the madeleine tins with butter, then scatter them with a little flour.

BEAT THE EGGS IN A MIXING BOWL WITH THE SUGAR UNTIL THE MIXTURE IS LIGHT AND FROTHY. Add the other ingredients, one after the other, mixing in lightly with a whisk. Let the batter rest for 15 minutes.

HALF FILL EACH MADELEINE MOULD WITH THE BATTER, THEN BAKE FOR 8-10 MINUTES FOR LARGE MADELEINES, ABOUT 5 MINUTES FOR SMALL ONES, UNTIL THEY ARE NICELY PUFFED UP AND GOLDEN BROWN.

TAKE THE MADELEINES OUT OF THE OVEN AND LET THEM COOL COMPLETELY ON A RACK. Eat them quickly!

× CHOCOLATE CHIP ×
cookies

MAKES ABOUT 12 COOKIES / 10 MINS PREPARATION TIME / 1 NIGHT RESTING TIME / 15 MINS COOKING TIME

It would be impossible to leave out chocolate chip cookies. These are wonderfully big, soft and chocolatey!

125 g (4½ oz) lightly salted butter

75 g (2½ oz) demerara sugar

½ teaspoon natural vanilla extract

1 egg

250 g (9 oz/1⅔ cups) plain (all-purpose) flour

½ teaspoon bicarbonate of soda (baking soda)

175 g (6 oz) dark chocolate, roughly chopped

PLACE THE BUTTER, DEMERARA SUGAR AND VANILLA EXTRACT IN A MIXING BOWL, THEN BEAT TOGETHER WITH AN ELECTRIC BEATER BEFORE ADDING THE EGG. Sift the flour and bicarbonate of soda over the mixing bowl, still beating. Mix in the chocolate.

SHAPE INTO A BALL OF DOUGH AND WRAP IN PLASTIC WRAP. Let the dough rest overnight in the fridge.

THE NEXT DAY, PREHEAT THE OVEN TO 180°C (350°F/GAS 4). Line a baking tray with baking paper or a silicone mat.

DIVIDE THE DOUGH INTO A DOZEN OR SO GOLF-BALL SIZED BALLS. Place them on the baking tray as you go, spacing them out well.

BAKE THE COOKIES FOR 15 MINUTES, UNTIL GOLDEN BROWN. When they come out of the oven, let them cool on a rack before eating.

✕ **PEANUT BUTTER** ✕
cookies

MAKES ABOUT 20 COOKIES / 10 MINS PREPARATION TIME /
10 MINS COOKING TIME

A great classic. You'll find it very difficult to devour just one ...

200 g (7 oz) plain (all-purpose) flour	1 egg yolk
75 g (2½ oz/⅓ cup) caster (superfine) sugar	50 g (1¾ oz) lightly salted butter, softened
2 tablespoons crunchy peanut butter	

PREHEAT THE OVEN TO 180°C (350°F/GAS 4). Combine all the ingredients together in a mixing bowl and work them together with an electric beater until you have a smooth, uniform dough.

LINE A BAKING TRAY WITH A SHEET OF BAKING PAPER OR A SILICONE MAT. Shape the dough into walnut-sized balls, placing them on the baking tray as you go. Press them lightly with the back of a fork to mark them lightly.

BAKE THE COOKIES FOR 10 MINUTES, UNTIL GOLDEN BROWN. When they come out of the oven, let them cool on a rack before eating.

× OATMEAL ×
cookies

MAKES ABOUT 20 COOKIES / 10 MINS PREPARATION TIME / 1 HR RESTING TIME / 15 MINS COOKING TIME

An ideal recipe for breakfast or children's snacks (grown-up ones too!).

100 g (3½ oz) icing (confectioners') sugar
200 g (7 oz) lightly salted butter
225 g (8 oz) plain (all-purpose) flour
75 g (2½ oz/¾ cup) rolled (porridge) oats
1 teaspoon baking powder
150 g (5½ oz) chocolate, to decorate (optional)

PLACE THE ICING SUGAR AND BUTTER IN A MIXING BOWL, THEN BEAT TOGETHER WITH AN ELECTRIC BEATER UNTIL THE MIXTURE IS PALE AND FLUFFY. Next, add the flour, rolled oats and baking powder, mixing them in with a wooden spoon.

SHAPE THE DOUGH INTO A LOG WITH YOUR HANDS AND WRAP IT IN PLASTIC WRAP. Let it rest in the fridge for at least 1 hour.

PREHEAT THE OVEN TO 180°C (350°F/GAS 4). Line a baking tray with baking paper or a silicone mat. Slice the roll of dough into rounds about 1 cm (½ inch) thick and lay them on the tray, leaving plenty of space between them.

BAKE THE COOKIES FOR 15 MINUTES, UNTIL THEY ARE NICE AND GOLDEN BROWN. When they come out of the oven, let them cool on a rack.

IF YOU WOULD LIKE TO DECORATE THE COOKIES, MELT THE CHOCOLATE IN A MICROWAVE OR A DOUBLE BOILER (A MIXING BOWL PLACED OVER A SAUCEPAN OF GENTLY SIMMERING WATER), THEN MAKE ZIGZAGS OF MELTED CHOCOLATE ON THE COOKIES. Let the chocolate cool and set before eating.

✕ VANILLA SHORTBREAD ✕
thins

MAKES ABOUT 20 BISCUITS / 10 MINS PREPARATION TIME / 1 HR RESTING TIME / 20 MINS COOKING TIME

Thin, delicate biscuits, perfect for a chic five-o'clock tea.

325 g (11½ oz) plain (all-purpose)
flour
125 g (4½ oz) caster (superfine)
sugar
200 g (7 oz) lightly salted or
unsalted butter (or a 50/50
mixture of the two if you like)
2 egg yolks
1 teaspoon natural vanilla extract

For the icing (optional):
100 g (3½ oz) icing (confectioners')
sugar
Juice of 1 lemon

COMBINE THE FLOUR AND SUGAR IN A MIXING BOWL. Mix in the butter with
an electric beater, until the mixture looks like breadcrumbs. Make a
well in the centre and pour in the eggs, lightly beaten with the vanilla
extract. Mix everything together well.

**SHAPE THE DOUGH INTO A LOG WITH YOUR HANDS AND WRAP IT IN PLASTIC
WRAP.** Let the dough rest for at least 1 hour in the fridge (or overnight
if possible).

PREHEAT THE OVEN TO 180°C (350°F/GAS 4). Line a baking tray with
baking paper or a silicone mat. Slice the roll of dough into rounds
about 5 mm (¼ inch) thick and arrange them on the tray, spacing
them out well.

**BAKE THE SHORTBREADS FOR 20 MINUTES, UNTIL JUST GOLDEN AROUND THE
EDGES.** When they come out of the oven, let them cool on a rack.

**DECORATE THE BISCUITS BY DUSTING THEM WITH FINE SUGAR IF YOU LIKE OR
MAKE SOME ICING BY MIXING TOGETHER THE ICING SUGAR AND LEMON JUICE.**
Brush the icing on the biscuits and let it dry and set before eating.

62

· CHOCOLATE ·

Chocolat

103

× INTENSE GUINNESS CHOCOLATE CAKE ×
with chocolate icing
and fine sea salt

SERVES 8-10 / 15 MINS PREPARATION TIME / 1 HR 15 MINS COOKING TIME / 1 NIGHT + 30 MINS RESTING TIME

Here I offer a variation on the traditional cream cheese icing and its tartness with a recipe that is reminiscent of the head on a glass of Guinness: an all-chocolate cake with an intense flavour that is further accentuated by a few crystals of fine sea salt.

For the cake:

125 g (4½ oz) unsalted butter

125 g (4½ oz) lightly salted butter

250 ml (9 fl oz) Guinness

75 g (2½ oz/⅔ cup) unsweetened cocoa powder

2 eggs

150 g (5½ fl oz) crème fraîche

1 teaspoon natural vanilla extract

275 g (9¾ oz) plain (all-purpose) flour

1 teaspoon baking powder

350 g (12 oz) caster (superfine) sugar

For the icing:

175 g (6 oz) good quality dark chocolate

75 g (2½ oz) unsalted butter

1 pinch fine sea salt

MAKE THE CAKE. Preheat the oven to 180°C (350°F/Gas 4). Place the butters and beer in a saucepan over a low heat. Sift over the cocoa and gently stir. Once the butter has melted, let the mixture cool for 5-10 minutes.

BEAT THE EGGS, CRÈME FRAÎCHE AND VANILLA EXTRACT TOGETHER IN A MIXING BOWL WITH A WHISK. Add the flour and baking powder, sifting them first, then the sugar. Finally, incorporate this mixture into the butter, Guinness and cocoa mixture.

BUTTER AND FLOUR A TALL 24 CM (9½ INCH) ROUND CAKE TIN AND POUR IN THE BATTER. Bake for 60-75 minutes. When the cake comes out of the oven, wait for 15 minutes before turning it out. Wrap the cake in plastic wrap and let it rest overnight.

THE NEXT DAY, MAKE THE ICING. Place all the ingredients in a bowl with 60 ml (2 fl oz/¼ cup) of water and melt them gently in a microwave or saucepan. Stir well until you have a smooth and glossy sauce, then let it cool and thicken slightly.

PLACE THE CAKE ON A RACK AND POUR THE CHOCOLATE ICING ON TOP. Use a flexible spatula to spread the icing all over the cake, including the side.

LET THE ICING DRY AND SET FOR ABOUT 30 MINUTES BEFORE SERVING.

✕ SWISS ROLL ✕
with dark chocolate icing and whipped mascarpone cream

SERVES 8 / 10 MINS PREPARATION TIME / 20 MINS COOKING TIME

A great classic to quickly master and devour!

For the genoise:

6 eggs

180 g (6½ oz) caster (superfine) sugar

50 g (1¾ oz) unsweetened cocoa powder

For the whipped cream:

250 ml (9 fl oz/1 cup) thin (pouring/whipping) cream, well chilled

2 tablespoons mascarpone cheese

For the icing (optional):

200 g (7 oz) dark chocolate

100 g (3½ oz) unsalted butter

MAKE THE GENOISE. Preheat the oven to 180°C (350°F/Gas 4). Separate the eggs. Beat the egg whites to soft peaks with an electric beater, then add 30 g (1 oz) of the sugar in three stages. Beat until the egg whites are very smooth and glossy.

IN ANOTHER MIXING BOWL, BEAT THE EGG YOLKS WITH THE REMAINING 150 G (5½ OZ/⅔ CUP) OF SUGAR UNTIL THE MIXTURE BECOMES PALE AND DOUBLES IN VOLUME.

SIFT THE COCOA POWDER OVER THE EGG YOLK MIXTURE AND MIX IN WELL. Gently fold in the beaten egg whites, lifting and turning the chocolate batter to keep as much air in the mixture as possible.

PLACE SOME BAKING PAPER OR A SILICONE MAT IN A GENOISE TIN WITH BUTTERED SIDES, THEN SPREAD THE CHOCOLATE BATTER ON TOP WITH A SPATULA. Bake the genoise for about 20 minutes. It should be dry but still spring back when you touch it with your finger.

TAKE THE GENOISE OUT OF THE OVEN, LET IT COOL SLIGHTLY, THEN COVER IT WITH A DAMP TEA TOWEL (DISH TOWEL) UNTIL IT HAS COMPLETELY COOLED. You can roll it up in the tea towel and leave it like that, which will make things easier when the time comes to finally roll it into a log.

MAKE THE WHIPPED CREAM. Whip the cream and mascarpone together until light, then spread it over the cooled genoise before rolling the cake up on itself, using the tea towel to help you hold and roll the cake up tightly.

TO MAKE THE ICING, MELT THE CHOCOLATE WITH THE BUTTER AND 80 ML (2½ FL OZ/⅓ CUP) OF WATER IN A MICROWAVE. Let the mixture cool before icing the cake. To ice, place the cake on a rack and use an offset spatula. Let the icing set and decorate the log however you like before enjoying!

THE ULTIMATE CHOCOLATE FUDGE CAKE
with cream cheese icing

SERVES 8-10 / 30 MINS PREPARATION TIME / 35 MINS COOKING TIME / 1 HR RESTING TIME

Much denser than my other buttermilk chocolate cake, the genoise in this cake has the added richness of chocolate and cocoa powder. You need a little dexterity to make this cake, but it is worth the trouble.

For the cake:

100 g (3½ oz) dark chocolate

180 g (6½ oz) plain (all-purpose) flour

100 g (3½ oz) unsweetened cocoa powder

2 teaspoons baking powder

100 g (3½ oz/1 cup) almond meal

200 g (7 oz) unsalted butter

275 g (9¾ oz/1⅓ cups) demerara sugar

4 eggs, lightly beaten

150 ml (5 fl oz) buttermilk

1 teaspoon natural vanilla extract

For the cream cheese icing:

100 g (3½ oz) chocolate, roughly chopped

300 g (10½ oz) cream cheese

100 g (3½ oz) unsalted butter, softened

725 g (1 lb 9½ oz) icing (confectioners') sugar, sifted

150 g (5½ oz) unsweetened cocoa powder

2 teaspoons natural vanilla extract

MAKE THE CAKE. Preheat the oven to 180°C (350°F/Gas 4). Butter two cake tins, 20 cm (8 inches) in diameter and about 4 cm (1½ inches) deep, then line the base with baking paper.

MELT THE CHOCOLATE IN A MICROWAVE OR DOUBLE BOILER (IN A MIXING BOWL PLACED OVER A SAUCEPAN OF GENTLY SIMMERING WATER). Sift the flour, cocoa and baking powder into a mixing bowl. Add the almond meal and combine.

IN ANOTHER MIXING BOWL, BEAT THE BUTTER WITH THE DEMERARA SUGAR UNTIL THE MIXTURE IS PALE AND DOUBLES IN VOLUME. Add the eggs one by one, beating between each addition. If the mixture curdles at this stage, add 1 tablespoon of the flour and cocoa mixture. Add the buttermilk, melted chocolate and vanilla extract. Mix together well, then gradually fold in the flour-cocoa mixture, lifting the batter with a spoon.

DIVIDE THE BATTER EQUALLY BETWEEN THE CAKE TINS AND BAKE FOR 30-35 MINUTES. The top of the cakes should be firm and rounded. To check whether they are done, insert the blade of a knife into the middle; it should come out clean.

TAKE THE CAKES OUT OF THE OVEN AND LET THEM COOL A LITTLE BEFORE TURNING THEM OUT ONTO A RACK TO COOL COMPLETELY. Once they are cool, remove the baking paper and cut them in half horizontally.

MAKE THE ICING. MELT THE CHOCOLATE IN A MICROWAVE OR DOUBLE BOILER (SEE RECIPE PAGE 72). Combine the other ingredients in a mixing bowl and beat using an electric beater, starting on a low speed. The mixture should be light and mousse-like. Add the melted chocolate.

USING A SPATULA, SPREAD ICING ALL OVER EACH CAKE HALF, THEN PLACE THEM ON TOP OF EACH OTHER TO BUILD THE CAKE AND ICE THE TOP. The quantities may seem enormous, but be generous! If you don't like icing as much as I do, halve the quantities and only lightly ice the cakes, just between each layer and on top. Let the cake rest for 1 hour in the fridge before serving.

✕ GUINNESS BROWNIES ✕

SERVES 8 / 10 MINS PREPARATION TIME /
25 MINS COOKING TIME

This is a variation on the famous brownie. Feel free to cover it with cream cheese icing (see recipe page 67) like its big brother, or to use another stout-style beer in place of the famous Irish champagne.

120 g (4¼ oz) dark chocolate	1 teaspoon natural vanilla
200 g (7 oz) unsalted butter	extract
80 ml (2½ fl oz/¼ cup) Guinness	150 g (5½ oz) plain (all-
6 eggs	purpose) flour
350 g (12 oz) caster (superfine)	50 g (1¾ oz) unsweetened
sugar	cocoa powder

PREHEAT THE OVEN TO 180°C (350°F/GAS 4). Break the chocolate into pieces and melt it with the diced butter in a microwave or double boiler (in a mixing bowl placed over a saucepan of gently simmering water). Let the mixture cool a little before adding the beer, then whisk together well.

BEAT THE EGGS WITH THE SUGAR AND VANILLA EXTRACT IN A LARGE MIXING BOWL UNTIL THE MIXTURE BECOMES PALE AND MOUSSE-LIKE. Add the melted chocolate and stir.

SIFT THE FLOUR AND COCOA TOGETHER, THEN ADD THIS MIXTURE TO THE PREVIOUS ONE, MIXING WITH A WOODEN SPOON.

BUTTER A 20 x 28 CM (8 x 11¼ INCH) RECTANGULAR CAKE TIN, THEN POUR IN THE BATTER. Bake the brownie batter for 25 minutes. It should still be a little soft and melting in the middle and a lovely crust should form on top.

✕ CHOCOLATE BAR CAKE ✕

SERVES 8-10 / 10 MINS PREPARATION TIME /
15 MINS COOKING TIME

Here's a recipe that's a little 'trashy', I admit, but very easy to make with just a few ingredients, all available from your local corner store.

225 g (8 oz) unsalted butter, at room temperature

225 g (8 oz) demerara sugar

4 eggs, beaten

1 teaspoon natural vanilla extract

225 g (8 oz) plain (all-purpose) flour

5 chocolate bars (whichever you fancy)

PREHEAT THE OVEN TO 180°C (350°F/GAS 4). Butter a baking dish or tray with sides measuring 20-28 cm (8-11¼ inches).

BEAT THE BUTTER WITH THE DEMERARA SUGAR IN A MIXING BOWL UNTIL IT BECOMES PALE AND LIGHT, THEN ADD THE EGGS AND VANILLA EXTRACT. Next, add the sifted flour.

POUR THE BATTER INTO THE BUTTERED DISH, THEN BAKE FOR 15 MINUTES.

MEANWHILE, CUT THE CHOCOLATE BARS INTO SLICES, OR 20 SMALL SQUARES IF USING A TRAY. You should have about 20 small squares small squares. Take the baking dish out of the oven and lay the pieces of chocolate bar on top of the cake. Return the cake to the oven to melt the slices of chocolate bar slightly.

TAKE THE CAKE OUT OF THE OVEN AND LET IT COOL AND SET BEFORE SERVING.

CHOCOLATE, PEANUT BUTTER
and Oreo® biscuit tart

× ×

SERVES 8-10 / 25 MINS PREPARATION TIME /
30 MINS COOKING TIME / 1 HR RESTING TIME

Perhaps the 'trashiest' recipe I have created in the last few years … But you have to let yourself go sometimes, my friends!

About 20 Oreo® cookies

175 g (6 oz) unsalted butter

400 g (14 oz) crunchy peanut butter

175 g (6 oz) icing (confectioners') sugar

200 g (7 oz) very good quality dark chocolate

FINELY GRIND THE COOKIES IN A FOOD PROCESSOR. Melt 75 g (2½ oz) of the butter and combine it with the cookie crumbs.

PLACE THIS MIXTURE IN THE BASE OF A ROUND 24 CM (9½ INCH) TART (FLAN) TIN (PREFERABLY LOOSE-BASED), THEN LET IT SET IN THE FRIDGE FOR ABOUT 30 MINUTES.

ONCE IT HAS SET, BEAT THE PEANUT BUTTER WITH THE SUGAR IN A MIXING BOWL. Spread this mixture over the tart base.

MELT THE REST OF THE BUTTER AND THE CHOCOLATE VERY GENTLY IN THE MICROWAVE (IN 30-SECOND BURSTS, STIRRING BETWEEN EACH ONE) OR IN A DOUBLE BOILER (IN A MIXING BOWL PLACED OVER A SAUCEPAN OF GENTLY SIMMERING WATER). Stir well until the chocolate is smooth.

POUR THE CHOCOLATE OVER THE PEANUT BUTTER. Let the tart set for 1 hour in a cool place, avoiding the fridge so the chocolate keeps its glossy appearance.

✕ CHOCOLATE CAKE ✕
with yuzu and ginger icing

**SERVES 8-10 / 10 MINS PREPARATION TIME /
30 MINS COOKING TIME**

Yuzu, a citrus fruit from Asia, is a fantastic substitute for lemon juice: it has a softer and sweeter flavour. It is becoming easier to find yuzu juice all the time, online or in specialist Japanese stores. You can also replace the pieces of preserved ginger with candied yuzu peel.

For the cake:	For the icing:
175 g (6 oz) plain (all-purpose) flour	3 tablespoons yuzu juice
4 tablespoons unsweetened cocoa powder	3 tablespoons icing (confectioners') sugar
225 g (8 oz) unsalted butter, softened	A few pieces of preserved ginger (in syrup if possible)
4 eggs	
225 g (8 oz) caster (superfine) sugar	

MAKE THE CAKE. Preheat the oven to 180°C (350°F/Gas 4). Combine the flour and cocoa in a mixing bowl, then mix in the butter, eggs and finally the sugar using an electric beater. Beat until you have a smooth, uniform batter.

POUR THE BATTER INTO A BUTTERED AND FLOURED ROUND 24 CM (9½ INCH) CAKE TIN, THEN BAKE FOR 25-30 MINUTES. Once the cake is well risen, insert the blade of a knife into the middle; the cake is cooked if it comes out clean. Once the cake is out of the oven, let it cool for a few minutes while you make the icing.

COMBINE THE YUZU JUICE WITH THE ICING SUGAR AND BEFORE THE SUGAR HAS TIME TO DISSOLVE, POUR THE ICING OVER THE TOP OF THE CAKE. Let it soak in. Once the cake has dried and cooled, the sugar will have formed a delicious crust.

DECORATE WITH PIECES OF PRESERVED GINGER AND SERVE.

75 • CHOCOLATE / *Chocolat*

✕ CHOCOLATE BANOFFEE PIE ✕
with (no churn!) rum and raisin ice cream and chocolate fudge sauce

SERVES 8 / 20 MINS PREPARATION TIME / 2 HRS 30 MINS RESTING TIME / 2 HRS FREEZING TIME

Yes, yes, all of that!

For the chocolate banoffee pie:

300 g (10½ oz) chocolate digestive biscuits (sweet wholemeal biscuits)

100 g (3½ oz) lightly salted butter, melted

2 tablespoons unsweetened cocoa powder

200 g (7 oz) caramel or dulce de leche (see recipe page 129)

3 medium bananas, fairly ripe

200 g (7 oz) dark chocolate, roughly chopped

300 ml (10½ fl oz) thin (pouring/ whipping) cream, well chilled

2 tablespoons mascarpone cheese

50 g (1¾ oz) icing (confectioners') sugar (optional)

Grated dark chocolate, to decorate

For the rum and raisin ice cream:

120 g (4¼ oz) sultanas (golden raisins)

100 ml (3½ fl oz) dark rum

4 eggs

150 g (5½ oz) caster (superfine) sugar

300 ml (10½ fl oz) thin (pouring/ whipping) cream, well chilled

For the chocolate fudge sauce:

300 ml (10½ fl oz) thin (pouring/ whipping) cream

250 g (9 oz) dark chocolate

50 g (1¾ oz) lightly salted butter, diced

START BY PUTTING THE SULTANAS IN THE RUM TO SOAK FOR 2 HOURS, THEN PREPARE THE BANOFFEE PIE. Crush the biscuits and combine them with the melted butter and cocoa. Cover the base of a 20–22 cm (8–8½ inch) round pie dish with this mixture. Place the dish in the fridge for 30 minutes to harden the base.

NEXT, SPREAD THE CARAMEL OR DULCE DE LECHE OVER THE BASE OF THE PIE (HEAT THE CARAMEL GENTLY IF NEEDED). Peel the bananas and slice them, then arrange them on top of the caramel or dulce de leche.

MELT THE CHOCOLATE IN A MICROWAVE OR DOUBLE BOILER (SEE RECIPE PAGE 72), THEN LET IT COOL. Using an electric beater, whip the cream, mascarpone and the icing sugar, if using, until light, then fold in the melted chocolate. Spread this cream over the bananas. Set aside in the fridge.

MAKE THE RUM AND RAISIN ICE CREAM. Separate the eggs. Beat the egg whites to fairly soft peaks with an electric beater, then add 100 g (3½ oz) of the caster sugar in two lots, beating well between each addition to make a firm and glossy meringue.

IN ANOTHER MIXING BOWL, BEAT THE CHILLED CREAM WITH AN ELECTRIC BEATER UNTIL LIGHT. Whisk the egg yolks with the remaining 50 g (1¾ oz) of sugar in a third bowl, until they are pale and mousse-like. Fold the egg yolk and sugar mixture into the meringue, then add the whipped cream and finally the rum-soaked raisins. Pour everything into a plastic container and let it set in the freezer for at least 2 hours (no need to whisk it in the meantime).

MAKE THE CHOCOLATE FUDGE SAUCE. Heat the cream in a saucepan or microwave, then add the chocolate, broken into pieces, and the diced butter. Stir to melt. Let the sauce cool slightly before serving with the ice cream and chocolate banoffee pie garnished with grated dark chocolate.

✕ BUTTERMILK CHOCOLATE CAKE ✕
with brown sugar and fine sea salt

SERVES 8–10 / 15 MINS PREPARATION TIME / 25 MINS COOKING TIME

In my first book I gave the recipe for Nathalie's chocolate cake, a dessert so good and so easy to make it has travelled around the world. This is its successor! It is true that this recipe is a tiny bit more technical, but we're all accomplished bakers afraid of nothing these days, aren't we? This cake has a dense and velvety texture without containing too much fat, because it doesn't have any cocoa butter, just cocoa powder. The buttermilk gives it a wonderful lightness and the combination of brown sugar and fine sea salt makes it simply addictive. To be adopted immediately!

170 g (6 oz) unsalted butter, at room temperature (not too hard, not too soft!)

140 g (5 oz/⅔ cup) caster (superfine) sugar

160 g (5½ oz) light soft brown sugar

3 eggs

2 teaspoons natural vanilla extract

210 g (7½ oz) plain (all-purpose) flour

120 g (4¼ oz) unsweetened cocoa powder

170 ml (5½ fl oz/⅔ cup) buttermilk

2 teaspoons baking powder

1 level teaspoon fine sea salt

PREHEAT THE OVEN TO 180°C (350°F/GAS 4). Butter a 22–23 cm (8½–9 inch) round cake tin, then line the base with a circle of baking paper.

MIX THE BUTTER AND THE TWO SUGARS IN A MIXING BOWL WITH AN ELECTRIC BEATER FOR ABOUT 2 MINUTES, UNTIL THE MIXTURE BECOMES PALE AND MOUSSE-LIKE. Add the eggs one by one, beating well between each addition and scraping down the side of the bowl. Next, add the vanilla extract.

SIFT HALF THE FLOUR AND COCOA OVER THE BATTER. Mix in with a spatula before adding the buttermilk. Then, add the rest of the flour and cocoa, the baking powder and finally the sea salt. Combine.

POUR THE BATTER INTO THE TIN AND BAKE FOR 20–25 MINUTES. To check whether the cake is done, insert the blade of a knife into the middle; it should come out clean.

WHEN IT COMES OUT OF THE OVEN, LET THE CAKE COOL FOR 5 MINUTES BEFORE TURNING IT OUT ONTO A RACK TO COOL COMPLETELY. The cake will be much better eaten the next day, so try to grin and bear it! If you live, you can cover it with icing (see recipe page 64) before serving.

× SHIRO MISO ×
brownies

SERVES 8 / 30 MINS PREPARATION TIME /
35 MINS COOKING TIME

I got the idea for these brownies from a recipe I read in the Wall Street Journal, which I have changed slightly. Shiro miso (white miso) is mild and gives a savoury hint to the brownies, which are usually very sweet.

200 g (7 oz) good quality dark chocolate

200 g (7 oz) unsalted butter

3 tablespoons shiro miso (white miso, a soya bean paste, from Asian food stores)

100 g (3½ oz) icing (confectioners') sugar

5 tablespoons plain (all-purpose) flour

4 tablespoons unsweetened cocoa powder

5 eggs

PREHEAT THE OVEN TO 180°C (350°F/GAS 4). Butter 20 cm (8 inch) rectangular baking dish or tin.

BREAK THE CHOCOLATE INTO PIECES AND DICE THE BUTTER. Melt them together with the shiro miso in a microwave or double boiler (in a mixing bowl placed over a saucepan of gently simmering water).

COMBINE THE SUGAR, FLOUR AND COCOA IN A MIXING BOWL, THEN GRADUALLY ADD THIS DRY MIXTURE TO THE MELTED CHOCOLATE, BEATING ALL THE TIME. Next, add the eggs one at a time, beating well between each addition.

POUR THE BATTER INTO THE DISH AND BAKE FOR 30-35 MINUTES. If you like your brownies nice and fudgy, don't cook them for any longer!

× CHOCOLATE AND ORANGE ×
polenta cake

SERVES 8-10 / 30 MINS PREPARATION TIME / 45 MINS COOKING TIME / 1 HR REFRIGERATION TIME

This rich and dense cake, with its chocolate ganache and orange icing is quite simply a 'killer'. Forgive me if there is a bit more washing up than usual, but this rather sophisticated cake is worth the trouble.

For the cake:

200 g (7 oz) very good quality dark chocolate

100 g (3½ oz) unsalted butter

100 g (3½ oz) lightly salted butter

3 tablespoons freshly squeezed orange juice (without pulp)

4 eggs

125 g (4½ oz) demerara sugar

1 heaped teaspoon baking powder

50 g (1¾ oz) instant polenta

Grated zest of 1 orange

For the icing:

50 g (1¾ oz/¼ cup) demerara sugar

Grated zest of 1 orange

100 g (3½ oz) dark chocolate

75 g (2½ oz) unsalted butter

Candied oranges or clementines

MAKE THE CAKE. Preheat the oven to 180°C (350°F/Gas 4). Butter and flour a round cake tin, 20 cm (8 inch) in diameter and 10 cm (4 inches) deep (straight-sided if possible).

PLACE THE CHOCOLATE, BUTTERS AND ORANGE JUICE IN A MIXING BOWL, THEN MELT THEM TOGETHER IN A MICROWAVE OR IN A DOUBLE BOILER (PLACING THE MIXING BOWL OVER A SAUCEPAN OF GENTLY SIMMERING WATER). Stir the mixture to make it smooth.

SEPARATE THE EGGS. Beat the egg whites to peaks with an electric beater, gradually adding half of the demerara sugar to make a firm and glossy meringue.

IN ANOTHER MIXING BOWL, BEAT THE EGG YOLKS WITH THE REST OF THE DEMERARA SUGAR UNTIL THE MIXTURE IS PALE AND MOUSSE-LIKE. Gradually add the melted butter mixture, then the baking powder, polenta and orange zest. Finally, using a spatula, gently fold in the meringue.

POUR THE BATTER INTO THE TIN AND BAKE THE CAKE FOR 40-45 MINUTES. When the cake comes out of the oven, let it cool completely in the tin.

MAKE THE ICING. Place all of the ingredients in a mixing bowl and heat them in a microwave or double boiler (in a mixing bowl placed over a saucepan of gently simmering water). Stir the mixture until smooth, then let it cool and thicken slightly.

UNMOULD THE CAKE, RUNNING THE BLADE OF A KNIFE AROUND THE SIDE OF THE TIN TO MAKE THIS EASIER, THEN COVER THE CAKE WITH ICING. Place the cake in the fridge for 1 hour to set the icing.

DECORATE THE CAKE WITH PIECES OF CANDIED ORANGE OR CLEMENTINE BEFORE SERVING.

✕ S'MORES PIE ✕

SERVES 6-8 / 30 MINS PREPARATION TIME /
2 HRS 30 MINS REFRIGERATION TIME

This is a typically American recipe, with the 's'mores' combination of digestive biscuits, chocolate and marshmallow, all in the form of a SUPER easy pie. The perfect dessert to finish a burger or hot dog night!

300 g (10½ oz) digestive biscuits (sweet wholemeal biscuits or chocolate biscuits)

75 g (2½ oz) unsalted butter, melted

250 ml (9 fl oz/1 cup) thin (pouring/whipping) cream

70 g (2½ oz) unsalted butter, cold and diced

350 g (12 oz) dark chocolate, roughly chopped

For the meringue:

2 egg whites

120 g (4¼ oz) caster (superfine) sugar

CRUSH THE DIGESTIVE BISCUITS AND COMBINE THE CRUMBS WITH THE MELTED BUTTER. Place this mixture in the base of a round spring-form cake tin, about 22 cm (8½ inches) in diameter. Place the tin in the fridge for about 30 minutes.

HEAT THE CREAM IN A SAUCEPAN. Put the cold diced butter and the chocolate in a mixing bowl and pour over the cream. Let the mixture rest for a few minutes before stirring together gently to make a smooth ganache. Pour this over the base of the tart and place the tin back in the fridge for about 1 hour.

MEANWHILE, MAKE THE MERINGUE. Beat the egg whites to soft peaks using an electric beater, then add the sugar in three stages, beating well between each addition. The meringue should be firm and quite glossy.

SPREAD THE MERINGUE OVER THE CHOCOLATE GANACHE. You can brown it with a blowtorch if you like. Let the pie cool for 1 hour in the fridge before serving.

✕ MOCHA DACQUOISE ✕

SERVES 8 / 30 MINS PREPARATION TIME / 1 HR COOKING TIME / 3 HRS REFRIGERATION TIME

Three layers of happiness!

For the biscuit:

6 eggs

325 g (11½ oz) caster (superfine) sugar

1 tablespoon unsweetened cocoa powder

175 g (6 oz) hazelnut meal

160 g (5½ oz) unsalted butter, softened

250 g (9 oz) dark chocolate, melted

30 ml (1 fl oz) very strong espresso coffee

For the coffee ganache:

180 g (6½ oz) dark chocolate

160 ml (5¼ fl oz) thin (pouring/ whipping) cream

30 ml (1 fl oz) very strong espresso coffee

1 tablespoon chocolate liqueur or Cognac

MAKE THE BISCUIT. Preheat the oven to 180°C (350°F/Gas 4). Separate the eggs. Beat the egg whites in a mixing bowl for 2 minutes, then add 170 g (6 oz) of the sugar, little by little, until you have a firm and glossy meringue. Fold in the sifted cocoa and hazelnut meal, lifting and turning the beaten egg whites with a spatula.

BUTTER THE SIDES OF A SPRING-FORM CAKE TIN, THEN LINE THE BASE WITH BAKING PAPER. Pour the hazelnut meringue into the tin. Even out the surface of the meringue and bake for 15–20 minutes. Take out of the oven and set aside.

BEAT THE BUTTER AND THE REST OF THE SUGAR IN A MIXING BOWL USING AN ELECTRIC BEATER, UNTIL THE MIXTURE BECOMES PALE AND DOUBLES IN VOLUME. Next, add the egg yolks, melted chocolate and coffee. Mix together well and pour over the semi-cooked meringue. Bake for another 25 minutes, until the centre of the cake is quite firm. Take it out of the oven, let it cool and place in the fridge for 2 hours.

MAKE THE GANACHE. Break the chocolate into pieces in a mixing bowl. Bring the cream and coffee to the boil in a saucepan, then pour this mixture over the chocolate. Let it stand for 1 minute before adding the liqueur and gently stir until the ganache is smooth.

POUR THE GANACHE OVER THE CAKE AND PLACE IT IN A COOL PLACE FOR AT LEAST 1 HOUR FOR THE GANACHE TO SET. When serving, unmould the cake and serve it with whipped cream and fresh raspberries if you like.

× NO-BAKE FIG, DATE AND PECAN TRAYBAKE ×
with chocolate and coffee ganache

MAKES ABOUT 30 SMALL SQUARES / 15 MINS PREPARATION TIME / 1 HR REFRIGERATION TIME / 1 HR RESTING TIME

This is another recipe in the little 'desserts-with-digestive-biscuits' series. You can make infinite variations of this recipe by adding dried fruit, marshmallows, milk chocolate icing, etc. But in my view the figs give the traybake a little 'crunch' that goes very well with the 'fudginess' of the dates. A rich and sweet dessert—in short, everything I love!

For the base:

300 g (10½ oz) digestive biscuits (sweet wholemeal biscuits)

7-8 soft dried figs

5-6 soft fresh dates (Medjool if possible)

120 g (4¼ oz) pecans, chopped

75 g (2½ oz) unsalted butter, melted

2 tablespoons unsweetened cocoa powder

For the ganache:

200 ml (7 fl oz) thin (pouring/whipping) cream

350 g (12 oz) dark chocolate, roughly chopped

1 teaspoon instant coffee granules

MAKE THE BASE. Crush the biscuits, then chop the dried figs and fresh dates. Chop the pecans as well.

COMBINE ALL THE INGREDIENTS FOR THE BASE TOGETHER, THEN LINE THE BOTTOM OF A RECTANGULAR 20 x 28 x 4 CM (8 x 11¼ x 1½ INCH) DISH WITH THIS MIXTURE. Place it all in the fridge for about 1 hour to harden the base.

MAKE THE GANACHE. Heat the cream in a saucepan. Put the chocolate and the coffee in a mixing bowl, then pour over the cream. Let it stand for 1 minute before stirring to make the mixture nice and smooth.

POUR THE GANACHE OVER THE BISCUIT BASE AND LET EVERYTHING COOL AND HARDEN IN THE FRIDGE FOR 1 HOUR. Cut the traybake into squares. Serve.

✕ CHOCOLATE AND COFFEE ICE CREAM CAKE ✕
with chocolate fudge sauce

SERVES 8-10 / 25 MINS PREPARATION TIME / 25 MINS COOKING TIME / 6 HRS FREEZING TIME

A densely chocolate dessert whose finishing touch is undoubtedly the aroma of the sauce.

For the ice cream:

300 ml (10½ fl oz) thin (pouring/whipping) cream

175 g (6 oz) sweetened condensed milk

2 tablespoons instant coffee granules

2 tablespoons coffee liqueur

For the cake:

225 g (8 oz) unsalted butter, softened

225 g (8 oz) caster (superfine) sugar

4 eggs

2 tablespoons full-cream (whole) milk

225 g (8 oz) plain (all-purpose) flour

3 tablespoons unsweetened cocoa powder

1 teaspoon baking powder

For the sauce:

150 g (5½ oz) dark chocolate

50 g (1¾ oz) lightly salted butter

250 ml (9 fl oz/1 cup) thin (pouring/whipping) cream

MAKE THE ICE CREAM. Combine all the ingredients in a mixing bowl and beat together with an electric beater until they have a lovely mousse-like consistency. Pour this mixture into a cold-resistant container and place it in the freezer for at least 5-6 hours.

MAKE THE CAKE. Preheat the oven to 180°C (350°F/Gas 4) and butter a 20 cm (8 inches) square cake tin with sides. Work the butter with the sugar in a mixing bowl using an electric beater, then add the eggs, milk, flour, cocoa and baking powder. Beat until the mixture is uniform.

POUR THE BATTER INTO THE BUTTERED TIN AND BAKE FOR ABOUT 25 MINUTES. To check whether the cake is done, insert the blade of a knife into the middle; it should come out clean. Once it is out of the oven, let the cake cool for a few minutes before turning it out to cool completely.

ONCE THE CAKE IS COOL, CUT IT IN HALF HORIZONTALLY. Take the ice cream out of the freezer and spread it on one of the cake halves. Place the second half on top and press down to fully enclose the ice cream. Wrap the cake in plastic wrap and place it in the freezer to firm it up well.

MEANWHILE, MAKE THE SAUCE. Break the chocolate into pieces and dice the butter. Put them in a mixing bowl. Bring the cream to the boil in a saucepan, then pour it over the chocolate and butter. Wait 1-2 minutes for the chocolate and butter to melt, then stir everything together.

BEFORE SERVING, DUST THE CAKE WITH ICING SUGAR AND COCOA IF YOU LIKE, CUT INTO THIN SLICES AND POUR OVER A LITTLE WARM CHOCOLATE SAUCE.

CHOCOLATE GALETTE DES ROIS
with tonka bean frangipane

SERVES 8 / 25 MINS PREPARATION TIME / 30 MINS COOKING TIME

After the end-of-year festivities, which are often particularly indulgent, I often have a little trouble appreciating the galette des rois. Fortunately, there are one or two recipes that are a little bit creative and manage to convince me ... This one, with chocolate and tonka bean, works well, but Gontran Cherrier's version, with kasha (toasted buckwheat) and candied grapefruit peel is a pure marvel. Until I manage to steal his recipe (are you listening, Gontran?), here is a galette I always enjoy making ...

For the crème pâtissière:

250 ml (9 fl oz/1 cup) fresh full-cream (whole) milk

3 egg yolks

50 g (1¾ oz) caster (superfine) sugar

25 g (1 oz) plain (all-purpose) flour

125 g (4½ oz) dark chocolate

1 tonka bean

For the frangipane:

125 g (4½ oz/1¼ cups) almond meal

2 whole eggs

75 g (2½ oz) unsalted butter, softened

40 g (1½ oz) caster (superfine) sugar

For the pastry:

2 rounds ready-to-use puff pastry

1 egg

Sugar syrup (see recipe page 230, optional)

MAKE THE CRÈME PÂTISSIÈRE. Heat the milk in a saucepan. Beat the eggs with the sugar and flour in a mixing bowl until the mixture is pale and doubles in volume. Pour the warm milk over the eggs and mix in. Return everything to the saucepan and heat it again, stirring constantly, until the custard thickens.

MELT THE CHOCOLATE IN A DOUBLE BOILER OR A MICROWAVE (SEE RECIPE PAGE 72). Stir the melted chocolate until smooth, then grate the tonka bean over the top. Stir to combine. Mix the melted chocolate into the crème pâtissière. Let it cool, with the surface covered with plastic wrap to avoid a skin forming on the surface.

MAKE THE FRANGIPANE. Beat the almond meal with the eggs, butter and sugar in a mixing bowl. Next, combine this frangipane with the crème pâtissière. Set aside.

PREHEAT THE OVEN TO 200°C (400°F/GAS 6). Lay one of the rounds of puff pastry on a baking tray, keeping its baking paper. Lightly beat the egg and brush it around the edge of the puff pastry; this will help it stick properly to the other sheet of pastry.

TOP THE PASTRY WITH THE FILLING, LEAVING A BORDER OF ABOUT 1 CM (½ INCH) AROUND THE EDGE. Place the second round of puff pastry on top and press the edges together to seal the galette well. Brush the galette with the rest of the beaten egg, then decorate the top of the galette however you like (you can make lattice patterns with a knife and/or brush with sugar syrup).

PLACE THE GALETTE IN THE OVEN AND IMMEDIATELY LOWER THE TEMPERATURE OF THE OVEN TO 180°C (350°F/GAS 4). Cook for about 30 minutes, until the galette is golden brown on top. Once it comes out of the oven, let it cool for 5 minutes before serving.

ALL HOME-MADE CHOCOLATE AND PEAR GENOISE,
for the best bakers

SERVES 8 / 1 HR 30 MINS PREPARATION TIME / 1 HR 20 MINS COOKING TIME / 2 HRS REFRIGERATION TIME

A labour of love, so take your time …

For the chocolate genoise:

200 g (7 oz) dark chocolate
225 g (8 oz) unsalted butter
6 eggs
225 g (8 oz) caster (superfine) sugar

For the poached pears:

6 firm pears
1 vanilla bean, halved lengthways

For the mascarpone cream:

4 egg yolks
4 tablespoons caster (superfine) sugar
150 ml (5 fl oz) marsala (sweet Italian wine)
500 g (1 lb 2 oz) mascarpone cheese

To assemble:

150 g (5½ oz) dark chocolate, grated
5 tablespoons very strong espresso coffee

MAKE THE GENOISE. Break the chocolate into pieces and dice the butter. Melt them in a microwave or double boiler (see recipe page 72). Stir until the mixture is smooth, then let it cool.

PREHEAT THE OVEN TO 150°C (300°F/GAS 2). Butter a spring-form cake tin, about 23 cm (9 inches) in diameter. Separate the eggs. Beat the egg yolks with the sugar in a mixing bowl until the mixture becomes pale and doubles in volume. Add the melted chocolate and mix in.

BEAT THE EGG WHITES TO PEAKS USING AN ELECTRIC BEATER, THEN GENTLY FOLD THEM INTO THE CHOCOLATE MIXTURE, LIFTING AND TURNING THE BATTER WITH A SPATULA TO KEEP AS MUCH AIR IN THE MIXTURE AS POSSIBLE.

POUR THE BATTER INTO THE TIN AND BAKE FOR 1 HOUR, UNTIL THE CAKE IS WELL RISEN. Take the genoise out of the oven and let it cool.

POACH THE PEARS. Peel the pears and put them in a saucepan with the split vanilla bean, cover with water and bring to the boil until the pears are very tender. Allow about 20 minutes. Let them cool in the poaching liquid before slicing them thinly.

MAKE THE MASCARPONE CREAM. Heat a saucepan of water. Combine the egg yolks, sugar and half the marsala in a mixing bowl. Place the mixing bowl over the saucepan of water and whisk for 5 minutes, until the mixture thickens and has the consistency of a sabayon.

BEAT THE MASCARPONE TO SOFTEN IT, THEN INCORPORATE THE SABAYON IN SEVERAL STAGES UNTIL YOU HAVE A SMOOTH, LIGHT CREAM. Place this cream in the fridge and let it cool.

ASSEMBLE THE GENOISE. Cut the cake in half horizontally. Spread a little mascarpone cream in the base of a dish, then cover with the pears and a little grated chocolate. Place one of the cake halves on top and sprinkle with a little coffee and marsala. Top with some mascarpone cream, then pears and chocolate. Cover with the second half of genoise. Sprinkle with the rest of the coffee and marsala, then spread the rest of the mascarpone cream on top.

LET THE CAKE REST FOR AT LEAST 2 HOURS IN THE FRIDGE (EVEN OVERNIGHT IF POSSIBLE).

✕ DARK CHOCOLATE MUFFINS ✕
with cream cheese icing and caramelised peanuts

MAKES 6 MUFFINS / 25 MINS PREPARATION TIME / 10 MINS COOKING TIME

This is a totally American combination, and it works beautifully!

For the muffins:

2 tablespoons unsweetened cocoa powder
100 g (3½ oz) plain (all-purpose) flour
50 g (1¾ oz) caster (superfine) sugar
1 egg
100 ml (3½ fl oz) full-cream (whole) milk
2 tablespoons sunflower oil

For the caramelised peanuts:

100 g (3½ oz) unsalted peanuts
100 g (3½ oz) caster (superfine) sugar

For the icing:

1 heaped tablespoon cream cheese
200 g (7 oz) icing (confectioners') sugar

Special equipment:

Muffin tin
Paper cases

MAKE THE MUFFINS. Preheat the oven to 180°C (350°F/Gas 4). Place the paper cases in the holes of your muffin tin.

SIFT THE COCOA AND FLOUR INTO A MIXING BOWL, THEN ADD THE SUGAR AND COMBINE WELL. In another bowl, beat the egg with the milk and oil, then pour this mixture over the flour and cocoa mixture. Mix together quickly without worrying about lumps, then divide this batter between the paper muffin cases.

BAKE FOR ABOUT 10 MINUTES, UNTIL THE TOPS OF THE MUFFINS ARE WELL RISEN AND CRACKED. Take the muffins out of the oven and let them cool completely.

MAKE THE CARAMELISED PEANUTS. Toast the peanuts in a dry frying pan, then add the sugar to caramelise them. Let them cool. If they stick together, break into pieces.

MAKE THE ICING. Beat the cream cheese with the icing sugar in a mixing bowl until smooth and creamy.

TOP EACH MUFFIN WITH ICING AND SCATTER WITH THE CARAMELISED PEANUTS BEFORE SERVING.

× CHOCOLATE WAFFLES ×

with whipped cream and Guinness-caramel sauce

SERVES 4 / 10 MINS PREPARATION TIME / 10 MINS COOKING TIME

A dessert that's creamy, crunchy and chocolatey all at the same time, with deep colours and malty aromas.

225 g (8 oz) plain (all-purpose) flour

40 g (1½ oz/⅓ cup) unsweetened cocoa powder

2 teaspoons baking powder

50 g (1¾ oz) caster (superfine) sugar

1 pinch salt

100 g (3½ oz) dark chocolate, finely grated

2 egg yolks

400 ml (14 fl oz) full-cream (whole) milk (or buttermilk)

125 g (4½ oz) unsalted butter, melted

3 egg whites

For the sauce:

100 g (3½ oz) soft brown sugar (vergeoise sugar or, if you can't find it, demerara sugar)

75 g (2½ oz) unsalted butter, softened

125 ml (4 fl oz/½ cup) Guinness

3 tablespoons crème fraîche or mascarpone cheese

Special equipment:

Waffle iron

SIFT THE FLOUR, COCOA AND BAKING POWDER INTO A MIXING BOWL, THEN ADD THE SUGAR, SALT AND CHOCOLATE. In another mixing bowl, beat the egg yolks with the milk, then pour them over the previous mixture, beating at the same time. Still beating, add the butter. If the batter seems too thick at this point, you can add a little more milk.

IN ANOTHER MIXING BOWL, BEAT THE EGG WHITES TO SOFT PEAKS USING AN ELECTRIC BEATER, THEN GENTLY FOLD THEM INTO THE WAFFLE BATTER.

PREHEAT THE WAFFLE IRON, REMEMBERING TO GREASE IT WELL (WITH OIL SPRAY OR BRUSHED WITH MELTED BUTTER). Pour a little of the batter onto the plates of the waffle iron and cook until the waffles are crunchy on the outside and melting inside. Keep in mind that your first waffles might fail because you will need to work out the right cooking time and temperature. Repeat until the batter runs out.

MAKE THE SAUCE. Heat the brown sugar in a saucepan until it simply dissolves, you don't need to caramelise it any further. Off the heat, add the butter and beer. Mix together well. Next, mix in the crème fraîche.

POUR THE HOT OR WARM SAUCE OVER THE WAFFLES AND SERVE WITH A LITTLE WHIPPED CREAM IF YOU LIKE.

× CHOCOLATE AND ALMOND ×
olive oil cake

SERVES 6 / 15 MINS PREPARATION TIME /
25 MINS COOKING TIME

A beautifully simple recipe for this wonderfully textured marvel!

150 g (5½ oz) very good quality dark chocolate	75 g (2½ oz/⅓ cup) caster (superfine) sugar
60 ml (2 fl oz/¼ cup) olive oil (not too strongly flavoured)	125 g (4½ oz/1¼ cups) almond meal
3 eggs	Fine sea salt

PREHEAT THE OVEN TO 180°C (350°F/GAS 4). Break the chocolate into pieces in a mixing bowl, then melt it in a microwave or double boiler (place the mixing bowl over a saucepan of gently simmering water). Add the olive oil and mix together well.

IN ANOTHER MIXING BOWL, BEAT THE EGGS WITH THE SUGAR UNTIL THE MIXTURE IS PALE AND HAS DOUBLED IN VOLUME. Add the almond meal, mixing at the same time, then add this mixture with the melted chocolate.

OIL (OR BUTTER) AND FLOUR A 20 CM (8 INCH) ROUND CAKE TIN, THEN POUR IN THE BATTER. Bake the cake for 25 minutes. The centre of the cake should stay soft and melting.

TAKE THE CAKE OUT OF THE OVEN AND LET IT COOL SLIGHTLY BEFORE UNMOULDING. Sprinkle with sea salt before serving.

OREO® COOKIE AND CREAM CHEESE
✕ *truffles with mocha milkshake* ✕

SERVES 4 / 15 MINS PREPARATION TIME /
1 HR REFRIGERATION TIME

This recipe is a total regression to childhood that's a little 'trashy' round the edges, but look, you're a responsible adult, aren't you?

For the milkshake:	For the truffles:
750 ml (26 fl oz/3 cups) fresh full-cream (whole) milk	250 g (9 oz) Oreo® cookies
125 g (4½ oz) dark chocolate	125 g (4½ oz) cream cheese
1 tablespoon instant coffee granules	1 tablespoon kahlúa (coffee liqueur), rum or Cognac (optional)
4 scoops ice cream (your choice of flavour–chocolate, vanilla, coffee, etc.)	unsweatened cocoa powder, to dust (optional)

START BY MAKING THE MILKSHAKE. Heat the milk in a saucepan, without letting it boil. Place 100 g (3½ oz) of the chocolate and the coffee in a mixing bowl, then pour over the hot milk. Stir and let it cool in the fridge for 1 hour.

MEANWHILE, MAKE THE TRUFFLES. Crush the cookies into crumbs and combine them with the cream cheese and liqueur, if using. Once this mixture is uniform, shape it into balls between the palms of your hands. If you like, you can also coat them in cocoa. Set them aside.

JUST BEFORE SERVING, POUR THE COLD CHOCOLATE-COFFEE MILK INTO A BLENDER WITH YOUR CHOICE OF ICE CREAM FLAVOUR. Blend to a thick liquid and pour into tall glasses. You can add a little more ice cream if you like. Grate the remaining chocolate and sprinkle on top of the milkshakes.

SERVE THE MOCHA MILKSHAKES WITH THE OREO CREAM CHEESE TRUFFLES.

creamy

CRÈME

creamy

BEURRE

106

· CREAMY ·

Crémeux

129

WHITE CHOCOLATE CHEESECAKE
with bourbon maple syrup

SERVES 8-10 / 30 MINS PREPARATION TIME / 3 HRS REFRIGERATION TIME

Oh yes, all that! To ensure the filling holds together well without using gelatine, it is important to use a very good white chocolate. It will be easier to work with. If the cheesecake seems too fragile to unmould, place it in the freezer for a little while and serve it frozen.

For the cheesecake:

350 g (12 oz) digestive biscuits (sweet wholemeal biscuits)
70 g (2½ oz) unsalted butter, melted
150 ml (5 fl oz) thin (pouring/whipping) cream
500 g (1 lb 2 oz) good quality white chocolate, roughly chopped
300 g (10½ oz) cream cheese
250 g (9 oz) mascarpone cheese

For the syrup:

120 g (4 ¼ oz) maple syrup
2-3 tablespoons bourbon

MAKE THE CHEESECAKE. Crush the biscuits in a small mixing bowl. Add the melted butter and combine, then cover the base of a tall round spring-form tin, about 25 cm (10 inches) in diameter, with this mixture. Place it in the fridge.

HEAT THE CREAM IN A SAUCEPAN, THEN POUR IT OVER THE CHOCOLATE. Let it stand for 1 minute before gently stirring to melt the chocolate and make a smooth ganache. Place this ganache in a cool place and let it cool completely.

ONCE THE GANACHE IS QUITE COOL, WHIP IT WITH AN ELECTRIC BEATER UNTIL LIGHT, ADDING THE CREAM CHEESE, THEN THE MASCARPONE, ONCE THE CREAM HAS STARTED TO HOLD ITS SHAPE. Beat together well.

SPREAD THIS MIXTURE OVER THE BISCUIT BASE AND SMOOTH THE SURFACE OF THE CHEESECAKE. Place in the fridge for 2-3 hours. Before serving, combine the maple syrup with the bourbon and serve this syrup alongside the cheesecake.

✕ VANILLA RICE PUDDING ✕
with Armagnac prunes

SERVES 6 / 10 MINS PREPARATION TIME /
1 HR 15 MINS COOKING TIME

A fabulous dessert for a long winter's evening.
You might want to skip the cheese course?

400 g (14 oz) pitted prunes

200 ml (7 fl oz) strong Earl
Grey tea, cold

150 ml (5 fl oz) Armagnac,
Cognac or Calvados

1 piece orange peel

1 vanilla bean

120 g (4¼ oz) short-grain rice

1 litre (35 fl oz/4 cups) fresh
full-cream (whole) milk

75 g (2½ oz/⅓ cup) caster
(superfine) sugar

PLACE THE PRUNES IN A SAUCEPAN WITH THE TEA, LIQUEUR AND ORANGE PEEL. Bring to the boil and simmer for about 30 minutes so the prunes are nice and soft. Cool.

PREHEAT THE OVEN TO 180°C (350°F/GAS 4). Butter a gratin dish measuring about 20 x 28 x 4 cm (8 x 11¼ x 1½ inches). Split the vanilla bean and scrape out the seeds with the blade of a knife.

COMBINE THE RICE, MILK, VANILLA SEEDS AND SUGAR IN A SAUCEPAN, THEN BRING TO THE BOIL. Pour this mixture into the gratin dish and bake for about 45 minutes so the rice is nicely swollen and very tender.

SERVE THE RICE PUDDING WITH THE COLD PRUNES.

✕ CHRISTMAS SYLLABUB ✕
with cumquat and cranberry compote

A great classic from home, and much nicer with this fruity accompaniment than with the traditional Christmas pudding. Thanks to Nigella for her festive inspiration!

For the compote:

200 g (7 oz) cumquats

80 g (2¾ oz) caster (superfine) sugar

250 g (9 oz) cranberries

For the syllabub:

2 tablespoons caster (superfine) sugar

Grated zest and juice of 1 lemon

Grated zest of 1 orange

2 tablespoons orange-flavoured liqueur (Cointreau or Grand Marnier)

350 ml (12 fl oz) thin (pouring/whipping) cream

MAKE THE COMPOTE. Prick the cumquats with a fork, then place them in a saucepan. Cover them well with cold water and bring to the boil. Drain and rinse them and repeat this process twice to remove the bitterness of these citrus fruits.

NEXT, BRING THE CUMQUATS TO THE BOIL AGAIN WITH JUST ENOUGH WATER TO COVER AND THE SUGAR. Stir to dissolve the sugar in the water. Simmer very gently, uncovered, for 15 minutes, stirring from time to time. Turn off the heat and allow the cumquats to cool.

TAKE THE CUMQUATS OUT OF THE SAUCEPAN AND SET THEM ASIDE. Add the cranberries to the syrup and bring to the boil. Reduce the heat and simmer for 7–8 minutes, until the cranberries burst.

WHILE THE CRANBERRIES COOK, SLICE THE CUMQUATS LENGTHWAYS AND REMOVE THEIR SEEDS. Combine them with the cranberries and let the mixture cool, stirring from time to time.

MAKE THE SYLLABUB. Combine the sugar, citrus zests, lemon juice and liqueur in a mixing bowl. Let the sugar dissolve. Add the cream, little by little, whisking until you have a soft whipped cream.

LET THE SYLLABUB REST FOR 3-4 HOURS IN THE FRIDGE BEFORE SERVING WITH THE CUMQUAT AND CRANBERRY COMPOTE.

✕ LEMON CHEESECAKE ✕

SERVES 8 / 30 MINS PREPARATION TIME /
3 HRS REFRIGERATION TIME

This is more like a Key Lime Pie with no chocolate. No baking in any case!

70 g (2½ oz) unsalted butter
200 g (7 oz) digestive biscuits
(sweet wholemeal biscuits)
Grated zest and juice of
2 lemons
135 g (4¾ oz) lemon jelly
(gelatine dessert) crystals

150 g (5½ oz) mascarpone
cheese
300 g (10½ oz) cream cheese
150 ml (5 fl oz) thin (pouring/
whipping) cream
candied lemon slices,
to decorate (optional)

MAKE THE CHEESECAKE. Melt the butter. Crush the biscuits in a small mixing bowl. Combine the melted butter with the crushed biscuits, then cover the base of a tall round spring-form cake tin, about 25 cm (10 inches) in diameter, with this mixture. Place it in the fridge.

HEAT THE LEMON ZEST AND JUICE IN A SAUCEPAN AND DISSOLVE THE JELLY CRYSTALS IN IT. Add a little hot water if you need to make up the liquid according to the packet instructions.

BEAT THE MASCARPONE AND CREAM CHEESE IN A MIXING BOWL WITH AN ELECTRIC BEATER TO SOFTEN THEM. Add the cream, beating on maximum speed, until the cream is smooth and fluffy. Combine the lemon juice–jelly mixture with the cream.

POUR THE FILLING OVER THE COLD BISCUIT BASE AND SMOOTH THE SURFACE. Let it rest for at least 3 hours in the fridge so the cheesecake is fully set. Decorate with slices of candied lemon if you like before serving.

× **GREEK YOGHURT WITH CINNAMON,** ×
coriander, brown sugar
and chocolate

SERVES 4 / 5 MINS PREPARATION TIME

More than a recipe, this is a delicious little
trick to have on hand in case of surprise
guests or when you need to keep things 'lite' ...

100 g (3½ oz) dark chocolate

2 teaspoons coriander seeds

1 teaspoon ground cinnamon

2 tablespoons soft brown
sugar (vergeoise sugar if
possible)

400–600 g (14 oz–1 lb 5 oz)
Greek-style yoghurt

BREAK THE CHOCOLATE INTO PIECES. Place all the ingredients,
except the yoghurt, in the bowl of a food processor and
crush them together, not too finely.

SCATTER THIS MIXTURE OVER BOWLS OF GREEK YOGHURT. You
can also use sheep or goat's milk fromage blanc.

× MATCHAMISU ×

SERVES 8-10 / 20 MINS PREPARATION TIME / 3 HRS RESTING TIME

Some purists would insist you make a matcha tea genoise from scratch for this dessert. I have saved you that step with a recipe that is much easier and quicker, but still full of flavour ...

3 egg yolks
60 g (2¼ oz) caster (superfine) sugar
225 g (8 oz) mascarpone cheese
50 g (1¾ oz) icing (confectioners') sugar
250 ml (9 fl oz/1 cup) thin (pouring/whipping) cream, well chilled
1 teaspoon natural vanilla extract
50 matcha green tea powder
About 12 ladyfinger biscuits (savoiardi)

BEAT THE EGG YOLKS AND CASTER SUGAR IN A MIXING BOWL UNTIL THEY ARE PALE AND MOUSSE-LIKE.

BEAT THE MASCARPONE WITH THE ICING SUGAR TO SOFTEN. Pour in the cream, little by little, then whip until light using an electric beater. Add the vanilla extract, then the egg-sugar mixture.

HEAT 125 ML (4 FL OZ/½ CUP) OF WATER IN A SAUCEPAN AND MIX IN TWO THIRDS OF THE MATCHA GREEN TEA POWDER, WHISKING VIGOROUSLY. Let the mixture cool slightly, then pour the tea into a dish.

QUICKLY DIP THE LADYFINGERS INTO THE TEA AND LAY THEM AS YOU GO INTO THE BASE OF A GRATIN DISH MEASURING AROUND 20 x 28 CM (8 x 11¼ INCHES). If there is any tea left over, pour it over the ladyfingers.

SPREAD OVER THE MASCARPONE MIXTURE AND LET IT REST FOR 3 HOURS IN THE FRIDGE. (Alternatively, use a smaller dish, divide the ladyfingers and mascarpone in two, and create two layers of each in the dish before refrigerating.) Before serving, decorate the 'matchamisu' with the rest of the (non-dissolved) tea.

MATCHA TEA PANNA COTTA
with milk chocolate sauce

SERVES 4 / 5 MINS COOKING TIME / 4 HRS REFRIGERATION TIME

This very chic dessert is a pretty colour combination and gives you a chance to use matcha green tea powder, which is sometimes difficult to work with.

For the panna cotta:

2 sheets gelatine

1 vanilla bean

350 ml (12 fl oz) thin (pouring/whipping) cream

2-3 tablespoons caster (superfine) sugar

100 ml (3½ fl oz) full-cream (whole) milk

About 2 teaspoons matcha green tea powder

For the chocolate sauce:

200 ml (7 fl oz) thin (pouring/whipping) cream

100 g (3½ oz) milk chocolate, roughly chopped

MAKE THE PANNA COTTA. Soak the sheets of gelatine in a bowl of cold water for a few minutes. Split the vanilla bean in two lengthways.

PLACE THE CREAM AND VANILLA BEAN IN A SAUCEPAN AND BRING TO THE BOIL. Remove from the heat before adding the sugar. Stir well to dissolve the sugar. Squeeze out any excess water from the sheets of gelatine and add them to the cream mixture. Stir until they have dissolved.

POUR THE MILK INTO A BOWL AND ADD THE MATCHA GREEN TEA POWDER. Whisk with a small metal whisk so the tea dissolves. Next, add this flavoured milk, little by little, to the cream, tasting the mixture as you go.

POUR THE CREAM INTO DESSERT DISHES OR RAMEKINS, THEN LET THEM SET IN THE FRIDGE FOR 4 HOURS.

MAKE THE SAUCE. Heat the cream in a saucepan, then pour it over the chocolate in a mixing bowl. Let it stand for 1 minute before stirring to melt the chocolate. Let the sauce cool (but not harden).

UNMOULD THE PANNA COTTA (SEE RECIPE PAGE 124), THEN SERVE IT WITH THE MILK CHOCOLATE SAUCE.

SAFFRON CRÈME BRÛLÉE WITH
blood orange sorbet and burnt butter biscuits

SERVES 4-6 / 2 HRS PREPARATION TIME / 6 HRS FREEZING / 2 HRS COOKING TIME / 1 HR REFRIGERATION TIME

This is an elegant and elaborate dessert. The three components can of course be served with other delights ...

For the crème brûlée:

250 ml (9 fl oz/1 cup) full-cream (whole) milk

1 large pinch saffron threads

10 egg yolks

175 g (6 oz) caster (superfine) sugar

750 ml (26 fl oz/3 cups) thin (pouring/whipping) cream

100 g (3½ oz) demerara sugar

For the sorbet:

Juice of 6-8 blood oranges (about 300 ml/10½ fl oz)

100 g (3½ oz) caster (superfine) sugar

For the biscuits:

225 g (8 oz) lightly salted butter

200 g (7 oz) caster (superfine) sugar

280 g (10 oz) plain (all-purpose) flour

Special equipment:

Ice cream maker (optional)

MAKE THE CRÈME BRÛLÉE. Preheat the oven to 120°C (235°F/Gas ½). Bring the milk and saffron to the boil in a saucepan, then take off the heat and let it infuse and cool.

BEAT THE EGG YOLKS AND CASTER SUGAR IN A MIXING BOWL UNTIL THEY ARE PALE AND MOUSSE-LIKE. Add the saffron-infused milk and the cream, whisking until the mixture is smooth and uniform. Strain the mixture and pour it into 4-6 ramekins.

PLACE THE RAMEKINS ON A BAKING TRAY AND BAKE FOR 1 HOUR AND 30 MINUTES, UNTIL THE CRÈMES ARE SET BUT STILL A LITTLE WOBBLY.

MAKE THE SORBET. Combine the orange juice with the sugar in a saucepan over a low heat to dissolve the sugar, then let the syrup cool completely and place in the fridge. Pour the syrup into an ice cream maker and start the churning cycle, then set aside in the freezer. If you don't have an ice cream maker, pour the syrup into an airtight plastic container and let it set for at least 6 hours in the freezer, stirring it with a fork at least once an hour to break up the ice crystals.

MAKE THE BISCUITS. Heat the butter in a small saucepan on a very low heat until it turns a nut brown colour. Pour it into a bowl and place in the fridge to harden. Once it is firm, place the butter and the sugar in a mixing bowl and beat with an electric beater for about 3 minutes, until pale and mousse-like. Add the flour and mix again.

SHAPE INTO A BALL OF DOUGH AND WRAP IN PLASTIC WRAP. Set aside in the fridge for at least 1 hour.

PREHEAT THE OVEN TO 180°C (350°F/GAS 4). Take the dough out of the fridge and divide it into small balls. Place them on a baking tray lined with baking paper or a silicone mat, spacing them out well. Bake for about 10 minutes, until the biscuits are nice and brown. Take them out of the oven and sprinkle with a little sugar. Let them cool.

SPRINKLE THE CRÈMES BRÛLÉES WITH DEMERARA SUGAR, THEN PUT THEM UNDER THE OVEN GRILL FOR A FEW MOMENTS OR CARAMELISE THE SUGAR WITH A BLOWTORCH. Serve them with the sorbet and biscuits.

✕ IRISH COFFEE CREAMS ✕

SERVES 6 / 30 MINS PREPARATION TIME / 2 HRS REFRIGERATION TIME

This ultra retro recipe (with its gelatine and cornstarch) comes from the inimitable Delia Smith. I have added some whiskey to make it a little less sensible and a little more my style ...

5 sheets gelatine

4 eggs

250 ml (9 fl oz/1 cup) full-cream (whole) milk

1 teaspoon cornflour (cornstarch)

6 teaspoons instant coffee granules

2 tablespoons whiskey

200 g (7 oz) crème fraîche

150 ml (5 fl oz) thin (pouring/whipping) cream, well chilled

For the coffee syrup:

175 g (6 oz) demerara sugar

3 teaspoons instant coffee granules

SOAK THE SHEETS OF GELATINE IN A BOWL OF WATER FOR A FEW MINUTES, THEN SQUEEZE THEM OUT WELL. Separate the eggs.

POUR THE MILK INTO A SAUCEPAN AND HEAT IT GENTLY. Beat the egg yolks with the cornflour in a mixing bowl. Once the milk has almost come to the boil, pour it over the egg yolks, whisking at the same time.

TRANSFER THIS MIXTURE TO THE SAUCEPAN AND ADD THE COFFEE AND GELATINE, ANY EXCESS WATER SQUEEZED OUT. Return the saucepan to a low heat and heat while stirring until the custard thickens. Let the mixture cool before adding the whiskey, then the crème fraîche.

BEAT THE EGG WHITES TO PEAKS USING AN ELECTRIC BEATER, THEN FOLD THEM VERY GENTLY INTO THE COFFEE CUSTARD. Divide the resulting mousse into tall glasses, cover with plastic wrap and place in the fridge for 2 hours.

MAKE THE COFFEE SYRUP. Heat the demerara sugar with 225 ml (7¾ fl oz) of water in a saucepan, then let it simmer for 15 minutes, until the sugar has completely dissolved. Melt the coffee in 1 tablespoon of hot water before adding it to the syrup. Let it cool completely in the fridge.

SERVE THE COFFEE CREAMS BY POURING A LITTLE COFFEE SYRUP OVER THEM, THEN TOP THEM OFF WITH THE CREAM, WHIPPED UNTIL LIGHT WITH AN ELECTRIC BEATER.

✕ PASSIONFRUIT ✕
panna cotta

SERVES 6 / 20 MINS PREPARATION TIME /
3 HRS REFRIGERATION TIME

This is a pretty recipe for adding colour to the immaculate white of the panna cotta.

4 sheets gelatine	100 g (3½ oz) caster
1 vanilla bean	(superfine) sugar
500 ml (17 fl oz) thin (pouring/	Juice and pulp of
whipping) cream	3 passionfruits

SOAK THE SHEETS OF GELATINE IN A BOWL OF COLD WATER FOR 5 MINUTES TO SOFTEN THEM. Split the vanilla bean lengthways and scrape out the inside with the blade of a small knife to get the seeds.

HEAT THE CREAM WITH THE VANILLA SEEDS AND BEAN IN A SAUCEPAN OVER MEDIUM HEAT, WITHOUT LETTING IT BOIL. Remove from the heat, then remove the vanilla bean before adding the sugar. Stir well. Squeeze out any excess water from the gelatine sheets and add them to the hot cream. Dissolve them, stirring, then let the cream cool.

PLACE SOME PASSIONFRUIT PULP IN THE BOTTOM OF EACH RAMEKIN OR SERVING GLASS. Pour the cream on top and place in the fridge for at least 3 hours (or overnight if possible) so the cream is fully set.

TO UNMOULD THE PANNA COTTA, WARM THE BOTTOM OF THE GLASSES OR RAMEKINS VERY GENTLY, THEN TURN THEM OVER ONTO EACH SERVING PLATE. You can skip this step by setting the cream directly in small glasses or serving bowls and pouring the passionfruit pulp over the top.

✕ LEMON CREAMS ✕
with honey biscuits

SERVES 4 / 20 MINS PREPARATION TIME / 2 HRS REFRIGERATION TIME

An elegant dessert for all occasions.

4 eggs

140 g (5 oz/⅔ cup) caster (superfine) sugar

30 g (1 oz) unsalted butter

Grated zest and juice of 2 lemons

300 ml (10½ fl oz) thin (pouring/whipping) cream, well chilled

6-7 honey digestive biscuits (sweet wholemeal biscuits, or the biscuits from the recipe on page 120)

LIGHTLY BEAT THE EGGS WITH THE SUGAR IN A MIXING BOWL. Pour them into a saucepan and add the butter and the lemon zest and juice.

PLACE SOME WATER IN A LARGE SAUCEPAN. Place the first saucepan inside the second one and heat until the water is just at a simmer. Cook the mixture in this double boiler for almost 15 minutes, constantly whisking, until the mixture thickens and resembles a crème pâtissière. Let it cool in the fridge for 2 hours.

BEFORE SERVING, WHIP THE CREAM USING AN ELECTRIC BEATER UNTIL LIGHT, THEN FOLD IT INTO THE LEMON CURD. Pour this cream into small dessert cups or bowls. Crumble the biscuits over the creams or serve them with the biscuits from page 120.

✕ DULCE DE LECHE ✕
(or confiture de lait in France!)

SERVES 4-6 / 20 MINS COOKING TIME

There are two ways of making dulce de leche. You can either simmer a can of sweetened condensed milk for 3 hours, submerged in a saucepan of water (be careful not to let the water evaporate), or follow the recipe below.

2 tablespoons demerara sugar

2 tablespoons lightly salted butter

395 g (13¾ oz) sweetened condensed milk

MELT THE DEMERARA SUGAR WITH THE BUTTER IN A SAUCEPAN. Pour in the condensed milk and heat, then lower the heat and let it simmer gently for about 15 minutes, until the mixture caramelises.

POUR THE DULCE DE LECHE INTO A CLEAN CONTAINER, DESSERT BOWLS OR RAMEKINS, THEN LET IT COOL BEFORE SERVING. You can also use it in other desserts, for example as a dip for the mini-choux on page 165.

132

· SOFT ·

Moelleux

169

✕ *THE* CARROT CAKE ✕

SERVES 8 / 10 MINS PREPARATION TIME / 45 MINS COOKING TIME

This is a revised version of the recipe from the Rose Bakery, the famous Parisian tea salon: I have added a dash of salt and cinnamon to soften the flavour of the cake.

For the cake:

5 carrots (about 100 g/3½ oz) each)

4 eggs

225 g (8 oz) caster (superfine) sugar

300 ml (10½ fl oz) sunflower oil

300 g (10½ oz) plain (all-purpose) flour

1 teaspoon five-spice mix (or cinnamon and nutmeg)

2 teaspoons baking powder

150 g (5½ oz/1¼ cup) finely chopped walnuts

For the icing:

125 g (4½ oz) lightly salted butter

250 g (9 oz) cream cheese

100 g (3½ oz) icing (confectioners') sugar

½ teaspoon natural vanilla extract

MAKE THE CAKE. Preheat the oven to 180°C (350°F/Gas 4). Butter and flour a 22 cm (8½ inch) round cake tin. Peel and finely grate the carrots.

BEAT THE EGGS AND SUGAR IN A MIXING BOWL UNTIL PALE AND DOUBLED IN VOLUME. Gradually add the oil and beat for a few more minutes. Next, add the carrots, then the flour, spices, baking powder and finally the walnuts. Mix together well.

POUR THE BATTER INTO THE TIN AND BAKE FOR ABOUT 45 MINUTES. Check whether the cake is cooked by inserting the blade of a knife into the middle of the cake; it is cooked when the blade comes out clean. Unmould the cake and let it cool.

MAKE THE ICING. Combine all the ingredients in a mixing bowl and beat together until the mixture is creamy. Spread this icing over the cake and serve.

× STICKY DATE ×
pudding

SERVES 6-8 / 30 MINS PREPARATION TIME /
40 MINS COOKING TIME

For this recipe, you need one of the essential ingredients of British cuisine: bicarbonate of soda!

For the pudding:

175 g (6 oz) soft fresh dates (Medjool if possible)

1 heaped teaspoon bicarbonate of soda (baking soda)

75 g (2½ oz) lightly salted butter

80 g (2¾ oz) demerara sugar

80 g (2¾ oz) dark soft brown sugar (dark vergeoise if possible)

175 g (6 oz) self-raising flour

1 teaspoon natural vanilla extract

For the sauce:

500 ml (17 fl oz/2 cups) thin (pouring/whipping) cream

150 g (5½ oz) unsalted butter

150 g (5½ oz) dark brown sugar

PREHEAT THE OVEN TO 180°C (350°F/GAS 4). Bring 275 ml (9½ fl oz) of water to the boil, then pour it into a mixing bowl. Chop the dates, then soak them in the hot water. Let them cool before adding the rest of the pudding ingredients and beating them well with an electric beater to break the dates into tiny pieces.

BUTTER A BAKING TIN OR DISH AND POUR IN THE BATTER. Bake the pudding for 40 minutes, then take the dish out of the oven and preheat the oven grill.

BRING THE SAUCE INGREDIENTS TO THE BOIL IN A SAUCEPAN. Pour half over the pudding and place it under the oven grill, until bubbles form on top.

SERVE THE PUDDING WITH THE REST OF THE SAUCE AND, IF YOU LIKE, SOME CRÈME FRAÎCHE OR CLOTTED CREAM IF YOU HAVE IT ON HAND.

✕ YOGHURT CAKE ✕
with honey, rosewater and pistachios

I first tasted this cake (and stole the recipe!) in Ireland, visiting some friends who are fantastic bakers. This recipe comes from one of the books of the sweet and lovely Rachel Allen, the Irish fairy of home cooking.

For the cake:

225 g (8 oz) plain (all-purpose) flour

1 teaspoon baking powder

100 g (3½ oz) caster (superfine) sugar

75 g (2½ oz) almond meal

2 eggs

1 tablespoon honey

250 ml (9 fl oz/1 cup) plain yoghurt

150 ml (5 fl oz) sunflower oil

Grated zest of 1 lime

100 g (3½ oz/¾ cup) pistachios, chopped

For the syrup:

100 g (3½ oz) caster (superfine) sugar

Juice of 1 lime (or 2 limes if not very juicy)

1 teaspoon rosewater

MAKE THE CAKE. Preheat the oven to 180°C (350°F/Gas 4). Butter and flour a 20 cm (8 inch) round cake tin. Sift the flour and baking powder into a mixing bowl, then add the sugar and almond meal.

IN ANOTHER MIXING BOWL, WHISK THE EGGS WITH THE HONEY, YOGHURT, OIL AND LIME ZEST. Pour this batter into the bowl containing the dry ingredients and beat for about 1 minute, until the mixture is uniform.

ADD THE PISTACHIOS TO THE BATTER (RESERVE SOME FOR DECORATION) AND MIX WELL, THEN POUR THE BATTER INTO THE CAKE TIN. Bake for about 50 minutes.

MEANWHILE, MAKE THE SYRUP. Combine the sugar and 150 ml (5 fl oz) of water in a saucepan, then bring them to the boil and simmer until the syrup reduces by half. Let the mixture cool before adding the lime juice and rosewater.

CHECK WHETHER THE CAKE IS COOKED BY INSERTING THE BLADE OF A KNIFE INTO THE MIDDLE; IT IS COOKED IF THE BLADE COMES OUT CLEAN. Take the cake out of the oven and let it cool for a few minutes before pouring the syrup over the top. If you like, you can prick the cake in a few places to help the syrup penetrate the cake.

LET THE CAKE COOL COMPLETELY IN THE TIN, UNTIL THE SYRUP FORMS A LOVELY CRUST ON TOP. Decorate with a few pistachios and serve.

✕ COFFEE AND WALNUT CAKE ✕
with buttercream icing

SERVES 8-10 / 15 MINS PREPARATION TIME / 25 MINS COOKING TIME

This is a classic in the same category as the Victoria sponge cake (see recipe page 141). The combination of walnuts and coffee works particularly well, and the buttercream brings it all together perfectly ...

For the cake:

250 g (9 oz) plain (all-purpose) flour

1 level teaspoon baking powder

250 g (9 oz) lightly salted butter

4 eggs

250 g (9 oz) demerara sugar

1 tablespoon very strong coffee (instant coffee is easier)

Walnut kernels, to decorate

For the icing:

100 g (3½ oz) unsalted butter, softened

200 g (7 oz) cream cheese

150 g (5½ oz) icing (confectioners') sugar

½ teaspoon natural vanilla extract

MAKE THE CAKE. Preheat the oven to 180°C (350°F/Gas 4). Combine the flour and baking powder in a mixing bowl. Mix in the butter with an electric beater, then the eggs, demerara sugar and coffee. Keep beating for about 1 minute until the batter is smooth and uniform.

POUR THE BATTER INTO A BUTTERED AND FLOURED ROUND 24 CM (9½ INCH) CAKE TIN. Bake for about 25 minutes. The top of the cake should be well rounded and golden. When it comes out of the oven, let the cake cool for a few minutes before unmoulding it, then let it cool completely.

MEANWHILE, BEAT TOGETHER THE ICING INGREDIENTS UNTIL YOU HAVE A LIGHT AND FLUFFY CREAM.

CUT THE CAKE IN HALF HORIZONTALLY. Spread half the icing over the lower half of the cake. Cover with the second cake half to make a 'sandwich', then ice the top with the rest of the buttercream icing. Decorate with walnut kernels before serving.

✕ VICTORIA SPONGE CAKE ✕

The Victoria sponge is THE most typical cake of the famous English afternoon tea, to be enjoyed after a game of cricket or croquet on a verdant lawn. Be careful not to confuse it with a genoise! The cake should be quite buttery, but its texture shouldn't be too dense. When it comes to the filling, you can use whipped cream (perfect in summer with a few pieces of strawberry or some raspberries) or a buttercream filling. As for the raspberry jam, it is non-negotiable. As always, I prefer a lightly salted butter. In this recipe, you can save it for the buttercream filling and use unsalted butter for the cake.

For the cake:

175 g (6 oz) plain (all-purpose) flour

1 teaspoon baking powder

4 medium eggs (or 3 extra large)

175 g (6 oz) caster (superfine) sugar

175 g (6 oz) unsalted butter, softened

Fresh berries, to decorate (optional)

For the filling:

150 g (5½ oz) lightly salted butter

350 g (12 oz) icing (confectioners') sugar

½ teaspoon natural vanilla extract

4 tablespoons raspberry jam

MAKE THE CAKE. Preheat the oven to 180°C (350°F/Gas 4). Sift the flour and baking powder into a mixing bowl, holding the sifter as high as possible to get plenty of air into your mixture. Add all of the other cake ingredients and beat for about 1 minute, until you have a smooth and uniform batter. The mixture needs to fall easily from a wooden spoon. If it seems a little too heavy, add 1 tablespoon of milk and beat for a few more seconds.

BUTTER AND FLOUR TWO ROUND CAKE TINS, 20 CM (8 INCHES) ACROSS AND 4 CM (1½ INCHES) HIGH. Divide the batter between them. Smooth them on top and bake for 30-35 minutes, without opening the oven door. To test whether they are cooked, touch the top of the cakes with your fingers; if they spring back to the touch, they are ready.

TAKE THE CAKES OUT OF THE OVEN AND LET THEM REST FOR ABOUT 1 MINUTE BEFORE UNMOULDING THEM (RUN A KNIFE BETWEEN THE CAKE AND THE SIDE OF THE TINS TO MAKE IT EASIER). Let them cool completely.

MAKE THE FILLING. Beat the butter with the icing sugar and vanilla extract in a mixing bowl until light and fluffy. Spread this cream on one of the cakes. Spread raspberry jam on the other one. Place the cake with jam on top of the one with the vanilla buttercream. Serve with extra icing sugar and fresh berries on top if you like.

✕ PINE NUT, ALMOND, ✕
lemon and ricotta cake

SERVES 8 / 20 MINS PREPARATION TIME /
1 HR COOKING TIME

This is a very moist and aromatic cake, with the added benefit of being gluten-free ...

225 g (8 oz) whole blanched almonds

50 g (1¾ oz) pine nuts

175 g (6 oz) unsalted butter, softened

200 g (7 oz) caster (superfine) sugar

3 eggs, beaten

Grated zest and juice of 1 lemon

1 level teaspoon baking powder

150 g (5½ oz) ricotta cheese, lightly beaten

PREHEAT THE OVEN TO 160°C (315°F/GAS 2–3). Butter and flour a round 22 cm (8½ inch) spring-form cake tin.

TOAST THE ALMONDS AND PINE NUTS IN A DRY FRYING PAN OR UNDER THE GRILL OF THE OVEN ON A BAKING TRAY. Let them cool completely, then finely grind them in a food processor.

BEAT THE BUTTER WITH THE SUGAR IN A MIXING BOWL USING AN ELECTRIC BEATER, UNTIL THE MIXTURE IS PALE AND DOUBLES IN VOLUME.

ADD THE ALMOND MEAL ALMONDS AND PINE NUTS. Mix together. Next, gradually add the eggs, the lemon zest and juice, then the baking powder. Finally, add the lightly beaten ricotta. Combine.

POUR THE BATTER INTO THE TIN AND BAKE FOR 50–60 MINUTES. When it comes out of the oven, let the cake cool a little before unmoulding.

DATE, BANANA AND HONEY CAKE
with whiskey icing

SERVES 8 / 10 MINS PREPARATION TIME / 1 HR COOKING TIME / 1 HR RESTING TIME

This is the 'adult' version of a rich and moist cake that is too often relegated to children's lunch boxes. If you feel so inclined, you can replace the butter and whiskey icing with a lemon and rum icing.

For the cake:

120 g (4¼ oz) soft fresh dates (Medjool if possible)

300 g (10½ oz) very ripe bananas

225 g (8 oz/1½ cups) plain (all-purpose) flour

1 level teaspoon self-raising flour

100 g (3½ oz) muscovado sugar (whole cane sugar)

175 g (6 oz) lightly salted butter, softened

3 tablespoons honey

2 eggs, beaten

For the icing:

50 g (1¾ oz) butter

200 g (7 oz) icing (confectioners') sugar

1 teaspoon natural vanilla extract

30-50 ml (1-1½ fl oz) whiskey or bourbon

MAKE THE CAKE. Preheat the oven to 160°C (315°F/Gas 2-3). Butter and flour a medium-sized loaf (bar) tin. Cut the dates into small pieces. Peel the bananas and mash them with a fork.

COMBINE THE FLOURS AND MUSCOVADO SUGAR IN A MIXING BOWL, THEN ADD THE SOFTENED BUTTER, HONEY AND EGGS. Beat for 2-3 minutes, until the mixture is quite uniform. Next, add the dates and mashed bananas. Mix together well.

POUR THE BATTER INTO THE LOAF TIN AND BAKE FOR 1 HOUR. To check whether the cake is done, insert the blade of a knife into the middle; it should come out clean. Take the cake out of the oven and let it cool slightly while you make the icing.

MELT THE BUTTER AND POUR IT INTO A MIXING BOWL CONTAINING THE ICING SUGAR AND VANILLA EXTRACT. Beat everything together well before adding the whiskey, which will give the right consistency to the icing.

COVER THE CAKE WITH ICING, WITHOUT TAKING THE CAKE OUT OF ITS TIN, THEN LET IT COOL AND ABSORB THE ICING. Serve the cake once it is cold and the icing is dry.

✕ ANGEL CAKE ✕

SERVES 6-8 / 20 MINS PREPARATION TIME / 40 MINS COOKING TIME

This ethereal cake comes straight from the United States, and I've given you the traditional recipe here. To achieve the very light texture of this cake, you need to find some cream of tartar (in specialist cake stores or online).

6 egg whites

1 pinch salt

1 tablespoon lemon juice

1 level teaspoon cream of tartar

150 g (5½ oz) caster (superfine) sugar

1 teaspoon natural vanilla extract

60 g (2¼ oz) plain (all-purpose) flour

Diced pineapple and strawberries, to decorate (optional)

whipped cream, to serve (optional)

TAKE A ROUND CAKE TIN, 22 CM (8½ INCHES) IN DIAMETER WITH 10 CM (4 INCH) HIGH STRAIGHT SIDES, AND LINE IT WITH BAKING PAPER. Be careful not to butter the tin or use a silicone mould, or you could ruin the cake: it will have trouble rising because the batter won't stick to the side of the tin. (Alternatively, use two smaller cake tins and check the cakes are ready a little earlier when cooking.)

PREHEAT THE OVEN TO 190°C (375°F/GAS 5). Using an electric beater, beat together the egg whites, salt and a few drops of lemon juice, until they are frothy, without being too firm.

ADD THE CREAM OF TARTAR AND BEAT AGAIN UNTIL THE WHITES START TO HOLD THEIR SHAPE. Gently incorporate the sugar, beating at the same time for about 2 minutes. Next, add the vanilla extract and mix everything together well.

ONCE THE EGG WHITES ARE QUITE FIRM AND GLOSSY, GENTLY SIFT THE FLOUR OVER THE TOP AND FOLD IT IN GRADUALLY WITH A LARGE SPOON OR FLEXIBLE SPATULA. 'Slice' the egg whites in two and lift up to gently incorporate the flour.

POUR THE BATTER INTO THE TIN AND BAKE FOR 35-40 MINUTES. The surface of the cake should be golden and rounded (the top of the cake should spring back when you press it lightly with your finger).

TAKE THE CAKE OUT OF THE OVEN AND RUN A KNIFE AROUND THE SIDE OF THE TIN TO UNMOULD IT MORE EASILY. Turn the tin over onto a plate and let it cool for 10 minutes before unmoulding the cake completely.

SERVE THE CAKE WITH DICED PINEAPPLE AND STRAWBERRIES, AND WHIPPED CREAM IF YOU LIKE.

✕ CRÊPES SUZETTE ✕

SERVES 6 / 15 MINS PREPARATION TIME / 15 MINS COOKING TIME

Something to try at least once! Make sure you reduce the sauce to intensify the flavour.

For the crêpes:

120 g (4¼ oz) plain (all-purpose) flour

1 tablespoon caster (superfine) sugar

2 eggs, lightly beaten

200 ml (7 fl oz) fresh full-cream (whole) milk

Grated zest of 1 orange

50 g (1¾ oz) unsalted butter, melted

For the sauce:

50 g (1¾ oz) lightly salted butter

Juice of 3-4 oranges (about 150 ml/5 fl oz)

Grated zest of 1 orange

Grated zest and juice of 1 lemon

1 tablespoon caster (superfine) sugar

3 tablespoons orange-flavoured liqueur, such as Grand-Marnier or Cointreau (optional)

MAKE THE CRÊPE BATTER. Sift the flour into a mixing bowl. Add the sugar, then make a well in the middle and pour in the lightly beaten eggs. Whisk, using an electric beater, gradually incorporating the flour.

NEXT, POUR IN THE MILK, LITTLE BY LITTLE, CONTINUING TO BEAT. Beat until the batter is completely smooth. Finally, add the orange zest and the butter (reserve a little butter for cooking the crêpes).

HEAT A CRÊPE PAN AND GREASE IT WITH A LITTLE BUTTER, USING SOME PAPER TOWEL. Pour in a ladleful of crêpe batter, tilting the pan at the same time so it covers the whole base. Cook the crêpe until its edges start to colour, then slide a spatula under the crêpe and turn it over. Once it is equally brown on the other side, slide it onto a plate and keep warm. Continue until you have used up all of the crepe batter (you should have about a dozen crêpes).

MAKE THE SAUCE. Gently heat the butter in a frying pan, then add all the other ingredients (and the liqueur, if using), stirring with a wooden spoon. Let the mixture heat and gently bubble before placing the first crêpe in the sauce and reheating it.

FOLD THE CRÊPE IN HALF, THEN OVER AGAIN TO MAKE A FAN SHAPE. Move it to the side of the pan and continue with the other crêpes. Keep going until all of the crêpes are coated with sauce and folded up. Serve the crêpes in the pan.

IF YOU LIKE, YOU CAN USE THE LIQUEUR TO FLAMBÉ THE CRÊPES JUST BEFORE SERVING.

× FLUFFY AMERICAN-STYLE ×
pancakes

MAKES ABOUT 10 PANCAKES / 5 MINS PREPARATION TIME /
20 MINS RESTING TIME / 15 MINS COOKING TIME

A recipe for Sunday mornings and when getting over the night before. Learn it by heart!

150 g (5½ oz/1 cup) plain (all-purpose) flour

1 teaspoon baking powder

2 tablespoons caster (superfine) sugar

300 ml (10½ fl oz) buttermilk

2 eggs, lightly beaten

70 g (2½ oz) unsalted butter, melted, plus extra for cooking and serving

Maple syrup, for serving

PLACE ALL THE PANCAKE INGREDIENTS IN A MIXING BOWL AND BEAT THEM TOGETHER WITH AN ELECTRIC BEATER UNTIL YOU HAVE A SMOOTH BATTER. Let it rest for 20 minutes.

HEAT A LITTLE BUTTER IN A FRYING PAN. Pour a small amount of batter in the middle of the pan, without spreading it out too much so the pancake is plump and light. As soon as small bubbles appear on the surface, turn it over and brown it on the other side. Keep going until you run out of batter (you should have about 10 pancakes).

SERVE THE HOT PANCAKES STRAIGHT AWAY WITH BUTTER AND MAPLE SYRUP.

× CROISSANT PUDDING ×
with caramel and bourbon

SERVES 4 / 20 MINS PREPARATION TIME /
10 MINS RESTING TIME / 20 MINS COOKING TIME

A great classic from Queen Nigella, but made over in my style. It is perfect for using up sad abandoned croissants from Sunday brunch. If you're not brave enough to make the caramel sauce yourself, make a simple crème anglaise with a very small amount of sugar, then melt 2 tablespoons of salted butter caramel into the custard while it is still hot.

3 slightly stale croissants	3 eggs, beaten
125 g (4½ oz) caster (superfine) sugar	2 tablespoons whiskey, bourbon or rum (optional)
250 ml (9 fl oz/1 cup) thin (pouring/whipping) cream	1 tablespoon icing (confectioners') sugar

PREHEAT THE OVEN TO 180°C (350°F/GAS 4). Tear the croissants into pieces and place them in a gratin dish (or any other ovenproof dish), measuring about 20 x 28 cm (8 x 11¼ inches).

COMBINE THE CASTER SUGAR AND 2 TABLESPOONS OF WATER IN A SAUCEPAN. Heat to dissolve the sugar, then let it bubble until a caramel forms and turns a lovely mahogany colour. Heat the cream in another saucepan, then pour it over the caramel off the heat.

LET THE MIXTURE COOL A LITTLE SO THE HEAT DOESN'T COOK THE EGGS, THEN ADD THEM WHILE WHISKING AT THE SAME TIME. At this point you can add the whiskey, bourbon or rum, if you like.

POUR THIS CUSTARD OVER THE CROISSANTS AND LET IT SOAK IN FOR 10 MINUTES. Sprinkle with icing sugar and bake for 20 minutes. Serve hot or lukewarm.

✕ BRIOCHE FRENCH TOAST ✕
à la Cyril Lignac

SERVES 4 / 10 MINS PREPARATION TIME /
10 MINS COOKING TIME

A deliciously moist and beautifully golden piece of brioche ...

3 eggs
200 ml (7 fl oz) fresh full-cream (whole) milk
4 thick slices brioche
50 g (1¾ oz) lightly salted butter

1 tablespoon icing (confectioners') sugar
Salted butter caramel (see recipe page 22) and/or caramelised pears or apples (see recipe page 180)

BEAT THE EGGS WITH THE MILK IN A MIXING BOWL OR SHALLOW BOWL.

SOAK THE PIECES OF BRIOCHE IN THIS MIXTURE, JUST ENOUGH TO MOISTEN THEM WELL.

HEAT A KNOB OF BUTTER IN A HEAVY-BASED FRYING PAN, THEN BROWN THE SLICES OF BRIOCHE FOR A FEW MINUTES ON EACH SIDE. Sprinkle the brioche with icing sugar half way through cooking to caramelise it slightly.

SERVE THE BRIOCHE WITH A SALTED BUTTER CARAMEL SAUCE AND/OR CARAMELISED PEARS OR APPLES.

✕ WAFFLES ✕

Here are the only two waffle recipes you really need. The toppings are up to you!

Belgian waffles

SERVES 4 / 10 MINS PREPARATION TIME / 10 MINS COOKING TIME

4 eggs
250 g (9 oz) caster (superfine)
sugar
250 g (9 oz/1⅔ cups) plain
(all-purpose) flour
250 g (9 oz) unsalted butter,
melted
Special equipment:
Waffle maker

SEPARATE THE EGGS. Combine the sugar, flour and melted butter with the egg yolks in a mixing bowl. In another mixing bowl, beat the egg whites to soft peaks using an electric beater, then gently fold them into the batter.

BUTTER THE WAFFLE MAKER AND HEAT IT UP. Pour a little batter onto the waffle plate, close and cook the first waffles until they are nice and brown. Keep going until you run out of batter.

American-style buttermilk waffles

SERVES 4 / 5 MINS PREPARATION TIME / 10 MINS COOKING TIME

250 g (9 oz/1⅔ cups) plain
(all-purpose) flour
70 g (2½ oz/⅓ cup) demerara sugar
½ teaspoon baking powder
½ teaspoon ground cinnamon
½ teaspoon fine salt
4 eggs, beaten
125 g (4½ oz) unsalted butter,
melted
400 ml (14 fl oz) buttermilk

COMBINE THE FLOUR, DEMERARA SUGAR, BAKING POWDER, CINNAMON AND SALT IN A MIXING BOWL. Make a well in the middle and pour in the beaten eggs, butter and buttermilk. Gradually incorporate the dry ingredients using an electric beater.

BUTTER THE WAFFLE MAKER AND HEAT IT UP. Cook the waffles as indicated above.

× MARMALADE AND WHISKEY ×
bread and butter pudding

SERVES 4-6 / 10 MINS PREPARATION TIME / 45 MINS COOKING TIME

A comforting dessert, like eating a piece of marmalade toast by the fire.

50 g (1¾ oz) lightly salted butter, softened

8 slices stale sandwich bread

Around 375 g (13 oz/1 jar) orange marmalade

1 vanilla bean

500 ml (17 fl oz) thin (pouring/ whipping) cream

4 tablespoons caster (superfine) sugar

2 tablespoons whiskey

4 eggs

1 tablespoon icing (confectioners') sugar

BUTTER THE SLICES OF BREAD ON BOTH SIDES. Spread the orange marmalade on half the slices of bread, then cover with the remaining slices to make four sandwiches. Place them in an ovenproof dish.

SPLIT THE VANILLA BEAN LENGTHWAYS AND SCRAPE OUT THE SEEDS INSIDE WITH THE POINT OF A KNIFE.

WHISK THE CREAM WITH THE CASTER SUGAR, VANILLA SEEDS, WHISKEY AND EGGS IN A MIXING BOWL. Pour this custard over the bread and let it soak in for 15 minutes.

PREHEAT THE OVEN TO 180°C (350°F/GAS 4). Sprinkle the top of the pudding with icing sugar and bake for about 45 minutes, until the corners of the sandwiches are caramelised.

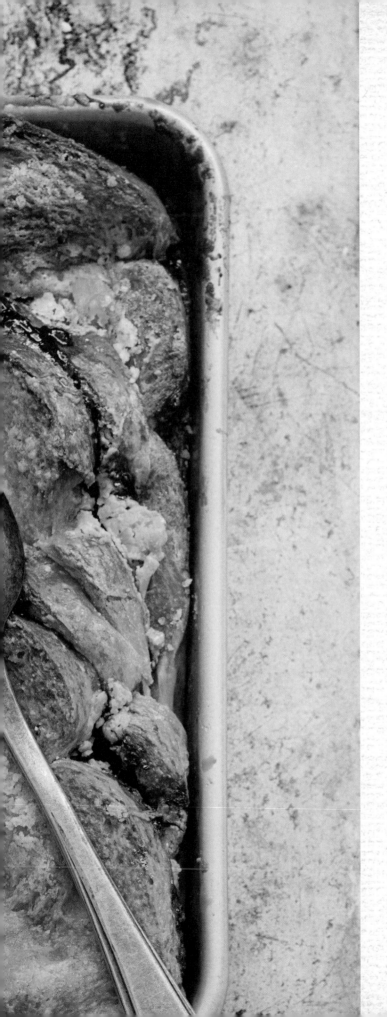

× PEANUT BUTTER AND JELLY ×
bread and butter pudding

SERVES 4-6 / 10 MINS PREPARATION TIME /
15 MINS RESTING TIME / 45 MINS COOKING TIME

Elvis would have loved it!

4 tablespoons lightly salted butter, softened

4 tablespoons peanut butter

8 slices stale sandwich bread

4 tablespoons blackcurrant, cherry, redcurrant or raspberry jelly

500 ml (17 fl oz) thin (pouring/whipping) cream

4 tablespoons caster (superfine) sugar

4 eggs

1 tablespoon icing (confectioners') sugar

SPREAD THE BUTTER AND PEANUT BUTTER ON FOUR SLICES OF THE BREAD. Spread the jelly on top of the peanut butter, then cover with the remaining bread slices to make four sandwiches. Place them in an ovenproof dish.

WHISK THE CREAM, CASTER SUGAR AND EGGS TOGETHER IN A MIXING BOWL. Pour this custard over the bread and let it soak in for 15 minutes.

PREHEAT THE OVEN TO 180°C (350°F/GAS 4). Sprinkle icing sugar over the top of the pudding and bake for about 45 minutes, until the corners of the bread are caramelised.

╳ TRES LECHES CAKE ╳

SERVES 8-10 / 20 MINS PREPARATION TIME / 35 MINS COOKING TIME / 40 MINS RESTING TIME

This is a recipe for a cake that is originally from Latin America, soaked in three milks and topped with cream. A dream cake, in other words ...

For the cake:

130 g (4½ oz) plain (all-purpose) flour

2 teaspoons baking powder

5 eggs

200 g (7 oz) caster (superfine) sugar

80 ml (2½ fl oz/¼ cup) full-cream (whole) milk

1 teaspoon natural vanilla extract

250 ml (9 fl oz/1 cup) evaporated milk

250 ml (9 fl oz/1 cup) sweetened condensed milk

65 ml (2 fl oz) thin (pouring/ whipping) cream

To decorate:

350 ml (12 fl oz) thin (pouring/ whipping) cream, well chilled

2 tablespoons icing (confectioners') sugar

Preserved maraschino cherries

MAKE THE CAKE. Preheat the oven to 180°C (350°F/Gas 4). Butter a baking tin or dish, measuring about 23 x 28 cm (9 x 11¼ inches). Combine the flour and the baking powder in a large mixing bowl. Separate the eggs.

IN ANOTHER MIXING BOWL, WHISK THE EGG YOLKS WITH 150 G (5½ OZ) OF THE CASTER SUGAR UNTIL THEY ARE PALE AND HAVE DOUBLED IN VOLUME. Add the milk and vanilla. Pour this mixture over the flour and gently mix it in to make a smooth batter.

BEAT THE EGG WHITES TO SOFT PEAKS WITH AN ELECTRIC BEATER, THEN POUR IN THE REST OF THE SUGAR. Keep beating until the egg whites form firm peaks. Fold them gently into the previous mixture, lifting and turning with a spatula.

POUR THE BATTER INTO THE BUTTERED BAKING TIN OR DISH AND BAKE FOR ABOUT 35 MINUTES. Check whether the cake is cooked by inserting the blade of a knife into the middle; it should come out clean. When the cake comes out of the oven, let it cool slightly before turning it out onto a rack, then place it in a rectangular dish, slightly larger than the baking dish, to cool completely.

COMBINE THE EVAPORATED AND CONDENSED MILKS WITH THE CREAM IN A BOWL. Prick all over the surface of the cake with a fork, then pour over this mixture so the cake can gently absorb it. Let it rest for 30-40 minutes.

MAKE THE CREAM FOR TOPPING THE CAKE. Whip the cream with the icing sugar using an electric beater until light. Spread this mixture over the cake, then return it to the fridge before serving. Decorate the cake with maraschino cherries (compulsory!) and serve.

CARAMEL MINI-CHOUX

with mascarpone dipping cream

MAKES ABOUT 30 SMALL CHOUX / 25 MINS PREPARATION TIME / 25 MINS COOKING TIME

A recipe that saves you the fiddly step of filling the choux by making them a tiny size for dipping in a cream rather than being filled.

For the choux pastry:

100 ml (3½ fl oz) fresh full-cream (whole) milk
90 g (3¼ oz) unsalted butter
1 pinch salt
1 pinch caster (superfine) sugar
110 g (3¾ oz/¾ cup) plain (all-purpose) flour, sifted
4 eggs, beaten

For the caramel:

200 g (7 oz) caster (superfine) sugar

For the whipped cream:

250 ml (9 fl oz/1 cup) thin (pouring/whipping) cream, well chilled
2 tablespoons mascarpone cheese
1 tablespoon icing (confectioners') sugar

PREHEAT THE OVEN TO 210°C (410°F/GAS 6-7). Make the choux. Start by combining the milk, butter, salt, sugar and 100 ml (3½ fl oz) of water in a saucepan. Bring to the boil, then let it simmer for about 20 seconds. Pour in all the flour at once and mix it in straight away, stirring vigorously with a wooden spoon. The mixture will be thick and lumpy at first, this is normal. Keep beating on the heat until the dough dries out a little and no longer sticks to the saucepan.

LET IT COOL FOR A FEW MINUTES BEFORE ADDING THE EGGS, ONE AT A TIME, STILL BEATING. (If your elbow is suffering too much, you can pour everything into a stand mixer and keep going that way!) Since egg sizes vary, check the consistency of the dough by running a finger through it: if the furrow closes in on itself straight away, the dough is ready and you can stop adding the eggs.

LINE A BAKING TRAY WITH BAKING PAPER OR A SILICONE MAT. Using a teaspoon, place small mounds of dough on the baking tray, leaving about 3 cm (1¼ inches) around each one.

IF YOU'D LIKE YOUR CHOUX TO BE SMOOTH AND GLOSSY, WET THE END OF YOUR FINGER AND PAT THE TOP OF THE CHOUX BALLS BEFORE BAKING. Let them cook for about 25 minutes, until the choux are puffed up and golden, then take them out of the oven and let them cool on a rack.

MAKE THE CARAMEL. Combine the sugar and 60 ml (2 fl oz/¼ cup) of water in a heavy-based saucepan, then place on the stove-top and heat to dissolve the sugar. Let it bubble until a caramel forms and turns a lovely mahogany colour.

ONCE THE CARAMEL IS GOLDEN BROWN, TAKE THE SAUCEPAN OFF THE HEAT AND, WORKING QUICKLY, DIP ONE END OF THE CHOUX IN THE CARAMEL. Place them immediately on the baking paper or silicone mat so they cool and set.

WHIP THE CREAM WITH THE MASCARPONE USING AN ELECTRIC BEATER UNTIL LIGHT, THEN ADD THE ICING SUGAR. Enjoy the caramelised choux dipped in the cream.

✕ FAIRY CAKES ✕

MAKES ABOUT 12 CAKES / 5 MINS PREPARATION TIME / 15 MINS COOKING TIME

Also known as cupcakes ...

For chocolate fairy cakes:

125 g (4½ oz) unsalted butter

125 g (4½ oz) caster (superfine) sugar

3 eggs

100 g (3½ oz) plain (all-purpose) flour

½ teaspoon baking powder

30 g (1 oz) unsweetened cocoa powder

For plain fairy cakes:

125 g (4½ oz) unsalted butter, softened

125 g (4½ oz) caster (superfine) sugar

3 eggs

100 g (3½ oz) plain (all-purpose) flour

½ teaspoon baking powder

1 teaspoon natural vanilla extract

For the buttercream:

150 g (5½ oz) unsalted butter, soft

250 g (9 oz) icing (confectioners') sugar

50 g (1¾ oz) unsweetened cocoa powder for the chocolate fairy cakes or ½ teaspoon natural vanilla extract for the plain fairy cakes

Special equipment:

Muffin tin

Paper cases

FOR THE BUTTERCREAM, BEAT THE BUTTER AND ICING SUGAR WITH AN ELECTRIC BEATER IN A MIXING BOWL UNTIL THEY MAKE A FLUFFY CREAM, THEN ADD THE COCOA OR THE NATURAL VANILLA EXTRACT. If you'd like to make two icings, divide the buttercream into two portions and add the cocoa to one and the vanilla to the other.

PREHEAT THE OVEN TO 180°C (350°F/GAS 4). Place the paper cases in the holes of a muffin tin.

MAKE THE FAIRY CAKES. Whip the butter with the sugar in a mixing bowl using an electric beater, then add the eggs, flour and baking powder, then the cocoa for the chocolate cakes or the vanilla extract for the plain cakes.

HALF FILL THE PAPER CASES WITH THE BATTER, THEN BAKE THE CAKES FOR 15 MINUTES, UNTIL THEY ARE WELL RISEN AND FIRM. Take them out of the oven and let them cool a little.

DECORATE THE CAKES WITH BUTTERCREAM USING A SPATULA OR PIPING BAG BEFORE SERVING.

Red miso buttercream

ENOUGH FOR 4 CUPCAKES / 3 MINS PREPARATION TIME

---

120 g (4¼ oz) unsalted butter, softened

1 tablespoon red miso (Japanese soya bean paste, from Asian food stores)

100 g (3½ oz) icing (confectioners') sugar

½ teaspoon natural vanilla extract

½ teaspoons grated zest of 1 lemon

COMBINE ALL THE INGREDIENTS IN A MIXING BOWL AND WHISK THEM TOGETHER WELL WITH AN ELECTRIC BEATER. The buttercream should be quite smooth and uniform. You can use this buttercream to fill and decorate the plain fairy cakes.

✕ LEMON CAKE ✕
with Cognac

SERVES 8-10 / 10 MINS PREPARATION TIME /
35 MINS COOKING TIME

The Cognac adds an irresistible little kick to this rich and dense cake. Served with lemon curd, it is divine!

For the cake:

100 g (3½ oz) lightly salted butter, softened

175 g (6 oz) caster (superfine) sugar

175 g (6 oz) plain (all-purpose) flour

1 teaspoon baking powder

2 eggs

3 tablespoons full-cream (whole) milk

1 tablespoon Cognac

For the icing:

125 g (4½ oz) icing (confectioners') sugar

Juice of 2 lemons

MAKE THE CAKE. Preheat the oven to 180°C (350°F/Gas 4). Beat the butter with the caster sugar in a mixing bowl, then add the flour, baking powder, eggs, milk and finally the Cognac. Beat for 1 minute with an electric beater until the mixture is creamy and uniform.

POUR THE BATTER INTO A BUTTERED AND FLOURED LOAF (BAR) TIN. Put the cake in the oven and bake for 35 minutes, until the top is firm and golden. To check whether the cake is cooked all the way through, insert the blade of a knife into the middle; it should come out clean. Take the cake out of the oven.

MAKE THE ICING. Mix the sugar with the lemon juice, then pour this syrup over the cake while it's still in its tin. Make sure you pour the lemon syrup over the cake while it is still hot! Let the cake cool and dry completely before turning it out and serving.

172

· FRUITY ·

Fruité

203

× BLACKBERRY AND APPLE ×
shortcake

Comforting and reinvigorating. Perfect for afternoon tea after a long autumn walk.

For the cake:

150 g (5½ oz) unsalted butter, cold

300 g (10½ oz/2 cups) plain (all-purpose) flour

1 teaspoon baking powder

100 g (3½ oz) caster (superfine) sugar

75 ml (2¼ fl oz) buttermilk

1 egg, beaten

For the filling:

3 tart cooking apples

1 tablespoon sugar

250 g (9 oz) blackberries

300 ml (10½ fl oz) thin (pouring/whipping) cream, well chilled

Icing (confectioners') sugar, to decorate

MAKE THE CAKE. Preheat the oven to 180°C (350°F/Gas 4). Cut the butter into small cubes.

PLACE THE FLOUR, BAKING POWDER AND BUTTER IN A MIXING BOWL AND WORK TOGETHER WITH AN ELECTRIC BEATER UNTIL YOU HAVE A MIXTURE WITH THE TEXTURE OF BREADCRUMBS. Next, add the sugar. Make a well in the middle and pour in the buttermilk and beaten egg. Work the dough together with your fingers (but not too much!) until you have a slightly sticky dough.

KNEAD THE DOUGH FOR ABOUT 1 MINUTE ON A LIGHTLY FLOURED SURFACE, THEN LAY IT IN A ROUND, BUTTERED 18-20 CM (7 x 8 INCH) SPRING-FORM CAKE TIN. Bake for 30-35 minutes, until the shortcake is golden and well risen.

MEANWHILE, MAKE THE FILLING. Peel the apples, cut them into segments and remove the seeds. Pour a little water into a saucepan, add the sugar and bring to the boil. Add the apples and poach them until they are very tender and the water has evaporated. Add the blackberries, crushing them slightly. Let this mixture cool.

USE THIS TIME TO WHIP THE CREAM UNTIL LIGHT USING AN ELECTRIC BEATER.

SLICE THE SHORTCAKE IN TWO HORIZONTALLY AND SPREAD THE WHIPPED CREAM ON THE LOWER HALF. Arrange the fruit on top, then place the top half of the cake on top of the fruit. Dust with icing sugar and serve.

× CLEMENTINE ×
syrup cake

SERVES 10 / 2 HRS 15 MINS PREPARATION TIME / 1 HR COOKING TIME

Another recipe that has travelled around the world as part of our current love for Yotam Ottolenghi and Mediterranean food, scented with rose and orange flower water. Here I have given you the basic version of this cake, which you can customise by adding pistachios, pomegranate seeds or exotically flavoured icings ...

For the cake:

1 orange and 2 clementines
(or 2 oranges)
6 eggs
250 g (9 oz) caster (superfine)
sugar
250 g (9 oz/2½ cups) almond meal
1 teaspoon baking powder
Rose petals and/or shelled
pistachios (optional)

For the icing:

Grated zest and juice of 1 lemon
2 tablespoons sugar

MAKE THE CAKE. Fill a large saucepan with water and bring it to the boil on the stove, then add the fruit and poach for 2 hours in the gently simmering water. Add more water during this time if needed. Drain the fruit and let them cool, then chop roughly and remove any seeds or pith. Purée in a food processor.

PREHEAT THE OVEN TO 190°C (375°F/GAS 5). Break the eggs into a mixing bowl. Add the citrus purée, then the caster sugar, almond meal and baking powder. Mix together well and pour the batter into a round 22 cm (8½ inch) spring-form cake tin.

BAKE THE CAKE FOR ABOUT 1 HOUR. Test whether it is cooked by inserting the tip of a knife into the middle; if it comes out clean, the cake is cooked. Remove it from the oven and let it cool slightly.

MEANWHILE, MAKE THE ICING. Combine the lemon juice and zest with the sugar. Pour this mixture over the still-warm cake and let it dry so the icing forms a crust on top of the cake.

YOU CAN DECORATE THE CAKE WITH ROSE PETALS AND/OR PISTACHIOS.

✕ ETON MESS ✕

with rose, strawberry and roasted rhubarb

**SERVES 6 / 10 MINS PREPARATION TIME /
20 MINS COOKING TIME / 2 HRS RESTING TIME**

Roasting the rhubarb intensifies its flavour and allows it to keep its shape.

---

250 g (9 oz) rhubarb	A few drops of rosewater
2 tablespoons demerara sugar	350 ml (12 fl oz) thin (pouring/
2 tablespoons freshly	whipping) cream, well chilled
squeezed orange juice	2 tablespoons mascarpone
200 g (7 oz/1⅓ cups)	cheese
strawberries	6 meringues

PREHEAT THE OVEN TO 180°C (350°F/GAS 4). Wash the rhubarb and cut it into sections about 4 cm (1½ inches) long. Place it in a gratin dish, then sprinkle with the demerara sugar and orange juice.

PLACE THE DISH IN THE OVEN AND ROAST THE RHUBARB FOR ABOUT 20 MINUTES, UNTIL IT IS VERY TENDER BUT HAS NOT LOST ITS SHAPE OR FALLEN APART.

MEANWHILE, WASH THE STRAWBERRIES, HULL AND SLICE THEM. Take the rhubarb out of the oven and let it cool slightly before adding the strawberries to the dish. Combine with the hot rhubarb and its cooking juices to poach them. Add a little rosewater and some demerara sugar if needed if the fruit seems very tart to you. Let the fruit cool for 2 hours.

WHIP THE CREAM WITH THE MASCARPONE USING AN ELECTRIC BEATER UNTIL LIGHT. Break the meringues into pieces and combine them quickly with the fruit. Divide this mixture between the serving dishes and drizzle with the fruit juices. Top with the whipped cream and serve.

✕ PASSIONFRUIT AND MANGO ✕
pavlova

SERVES 8-10 / 10 MINS PREPARATION TIME / 45 MINS COOKING TIME

Nothing goes better with this sweet dream than the tartness and crunch of passionfruit and the smooth touch of mango!

For the meringue:

4 egg whites, at room temperature

250 g (9 oz) caster (superfine) sugar

1 teaspoon white wine vinegar

½ teaspoon natural vanilla extract

2 teaspoons cornflour (cornstarch)

For the filling:

2-3 passionfruit

1 ripe mango

300 ml (10½ fl oz) thin (pouring/whipping) cream, well chilled

3 tablespoons mascarpone cheese

MAKE THE MERINGUE. Preheat the oven to 180°C (350°F/Gas 4). Beat the egg whites to soft peaks with an electric beater, then gradually incorporate the caster sugar.

ONCE THE SUGAR HAS COMPLETELY DISSOLVED AND THE MERINGUE IS SMOOTH AND GLOSSY, ADD THE VINEGAR, VANILLA EXTRACT AND CORNFLOUR. Mix together well.

PLACE THE MERINGUE IN A ROUND, HIGH PILE ON A BAKING TRAY LINED WITH BAKING PAPER OR A SILICONE MAT (MUCH MORE PRACTICAL IN THIS CASE). Bake for 45 minutes, then turn off the oven, open the oven door and let the pavlova cool completely.

MAKE THE TOPPING. Cut open the passionfruit and take out the pulp. Strain the pulp if you like to remove the seeds. Peel the mango and dice the flesh. Using an electric beater, whip the cream and mascarpone in a mixing bowl until light.

SPREAD A THICK LAYER OF WHIPPED CREAM ON TOP OF THE MERINGUE, THEN TOP WITH THE PASSIONFRUIT PULP MIXED WITH THE DICED MANGO. SERVE.

× APPLE CRUMBLE ×

with maple syrup, caramelised bacon and bay leaf crème anglaise

---

SERVES 6 / 20 MINS PREPARATION TIME / 45 MINS COOKING TIME

These elements go so well together! I tried a version of this dessert that mixed the bacon directly into the crumble, but the result wasn't as delicious as when the caramelised bacon is scattered over at the last minute. It is much tastier and more succulent that way. If you don't have an ovenproof cast-iron frying pan, pre-cook the apples in an ordinary frying pan, then make the crumble in a baking dish.

For the caramelised apples:

8-10 tart cooking apples, depending on how deep your dish is

75 g (2½ oz) unsalted butter

2 tablespoons sugar

3 tablespoons maple syrup

For the crumble:

225 g (8 oz/1½ cups) plain (all-purpose) flour

100 g (3½ oz) caster (superfine) sugar

175 g (6 oz) lightly salted butter, cold

For the crème anglaise:

200 ml (7 fl oz) fresh full-cream (whole) milk

300 ml (10½ fl oz) thin (pouring/whipping) cream

1 vanilla bean, halved lengthways

1 fresh bay leaf

5 egg yolks

100 g (3½ oz) caster (superfine) sugar

For the caramelised bacon:

120 g (4¼ oz) chopped bacon (lardons)

2 tablespoons sugar

PREHEAT THE OVEN TO 180°C (350°F/GAS 4). Make the caramelised apples. Peel the apples, seed them and cut them into segments. Melt the butter in a cast-iron frying pan, then add the apple. After 1 minute of cooking, sprinkle them with sugar. Let them caramelise a little, then pour over the maple syrup and stir. After cooking for 2 minutes, take the apples off the heat.

MAKE THE CRUMBLE. Place the flour, sugar and diced butter in the bowl of a food processor and process until the mixture resembles crumbs. Top the apples with the crumble and bake for about 45 minutes.

MEANWHILE, MAKE THE CRÈME ANGLAISE. Bring the milk to the boil in a saucepan with the cream, the split vanilla bean and the bay leaf. Beat the egg yolks with the sugar in a large mixing bowl until they are pale and have doubled in volume. Pour the contents of the saucepan over the eggs, stirring with a wooden spoon, then return everything to the saucepan. Heat over a low heat until the cream thickens, constantly stirring with the wooden spoon. Run your finger through the custard on the back of the spoon; if the trace left by your finger stays, the custard is the right consistency. Take it off the heat immediately and pour it into a cold container to stop the cooking process. You can leave the vanilla bean and bay leaf in the custard until serving time.

ABOUT 10 MINUTES BEFORE SERVING THE CRUMBLE, CARAMELISE THE BACON. To do this, heat a frying pan, add the bacon pieces and, once they start to brown, sprinkle them with sugar. The sugar will melt in the bacon fat (yum!) and caramelise everything.

TAKE THE CRUMBLE OUT OF THE OVEN ONCE IT IS GOLDEN ON TOP. Scatter over the caramelised bacon pieces and serve with the crème anglaise. If you would like to add a little hot-cold contrast, serve it all with a scoop of vanilla ice cream alongside.

✕ PEACH CLAFOUTIS ✕
with buttermilk sorbet and rosemary sugar

SERVES 6-8 / 15 MINS PREPARATION TIME / 45 MINS COOKING TIME / 1 HR CHURNING TIME

I have taken little ideas from here and there for this recipe: the almond meal from Éric Fréchon and the buttermilk, which makes the mixture light, is inspired by our American friends. Here I have chosen to combine the delicate, summery flavours of peaches and rosemary, which I am particularly fond of, but there is nothing to stop you using other fruits - raspberries, apricots, plums, blueberries, cherries, etc.

For the clafoutis:

100 g (3½ oz/1 cup) almond meal

6-8 blood peaches (depending on their size).

1 vanilla bean

2 whole eggs and 2 yolks

100 g (3½ oz) caster (superfine) sugar

20 g (¾ oz) cornflour (cornstarch)

150 ml (5 fl oz) buttermilk

150 ml (5 fl oz) full-cream (whole) milk

For the buttermilk sorbet:

75 g (2½ oz) caster (superfine) sugar

250 ml (9 fl oz/1 cup) buttermilk

1 teaspoon natural vanilla extract

For the rosemary sugar:

5 tablespoons caster (superfine) sugar

1 tablespoon fresh rosemary leaves

Special equipment:

Ice cream maker

MAKE THE CLAFOUTIS. Preheat the oven to 180°C (350°F/Gas 4). Sprinkle the base of a cake tin with some almond meal. Submerge the peaches in a saucepan of boiling water for a few minutes, then peel them, cut them into four and remove the stone. Roll the pieces of peach in the rest of the almond meal and arrange them tightly in the base of the tin.

SPLIT THE VANILLA BEAN AND SCRAPE OUT THE SEEDS WITH THE BLADE OF A KNIFE. Mix the eggs with the sugar and cornflour in a stand mixer, until the mixture is smooth and pale. Next, add the buttermilk, full-cream milk and vanilla seeds.

GENTLY POUR THE BATTER OVER THE PEACHES SO YOU DON'T DISTURB THEM TOO MUCH, THEN BAKE FOR ABOUT 45 MINUTES, UNTIL THE CLAFOUTIS IS NICELY PUFFED UP AND GOLDEN.

MEANWHILE, MAKE THE SORBET. Combine the sugar and 75 ml (2¼ oz) of water in a saucepan, then heat until the sugar is dissolved. Let this syrup cool. Combine the buttermilk with the sugar syrup until the mixture is creamy. Add the vanilla extract, then pour everything into the bowl of the ice cream maker and start the churn cycle. Once the sorbet is ready, serve it as soon as possible.

TO MAKE THE ROSEMARY SUGAR, FINELY GRIND UP THE SUGAR AND ROSEMARY IN A FOOD PROCESSOR.

ONCE THE CLAFOUTIS IS COOKED, TAKE IT OUT OF THE OVEN AND LET IT COOL SLIGHTLY. Serve dusted with rosemary sugar and accompanied by the buttermilk sorbet.

× PINEAPPLE TIRAMISU ×

with ginger, yuzu and whipped cream

SERVES 8-10 / 30 MINS PREPARATION TIME /
2 HRS REFRIGERATION TIME

In my family we call this dessert 'Beattie's thing, Beattie being my beloved 92 year-old aunt. It has all the ingredients of an Irish dessert from the 1970s: whipped cream, crushed biscuits with a hint of salt, acidic fruits ... And all that in 30 minutes flat! This is my updated version with yuzu (an Asian citrus fruit), ginger and a huge kiss to my beloved aunt.

About 350 g (12 oz) crunchy ginger nut biscuits

50 g (1¾ oz) lightly salted butter

400 g (14 oz) fresh pineapple (or tinned pineapple if you don't have fresh)

2 tablespoons preserved ginger in syrup

1 tablespoon yuzu juice

350 ml (12 fl oz) thin (pouring/whipping) cream, well chilled

2 tablespoons mascarpone cheese

2 tablespoons icing (confectioners') sugar

CRUSH THE BISCUITS IN A FOOD PROCESSOR OR BY PLACING THEM IN A TEA TOWEL (DISH TOWEL) AND CRUSHING THEM WITH A ROLLING PIN.

MELT THE BUTTER IN A SAUCEPAN OR THE MICROWAVE, THEN MIX WITH THE CRUSHED BISCUITS. Place this mixture in the bottom of a gratin dish about 20 cm (8 inches) wide and 28 cm (11¼ inches) long. Pack the mixture down well. Place the dish in the fridge so the biscuit base cools and hardens.

PEEL AND CHOP THE PINEAPPLE INTO SMALL CUBES. Combine it with the ginger and its syrup and the yuzu juice.

USING AN ELECTRIC BEATER, WHIP THE CREAM WITH THE MASCARPONE IN A MIXING BOWL UNTIL LIGHT. Add the icing sugar, still beating.

ONCE THE BISCUIT BASE IS QUITE COLD, COVER WITH PINEAPPLE, THEN TOP WITH WHIPPED CREAM AND LET IT REST FOR 1- 2 HOURS IN THE FRIDGE BEFORE SERVING.

✕ FREE-FORM APPLE PIE ✕
with spiced apple-caramel sauce

SERVES 8 / 25 MINS PREPARATION TIME / 1 HR REFRIGERATION TIME / 30 MINS COOKING TIME

No need for tins, dishes and all the washing up that goes with them for this recipe! This pie stands alone. The parts hidden under the folded pastry around the edge are nicely stewed and the middle is crusty. Add to this a spiced caramel sauce (from American chef Bobbly Flay) and you have a dessert that is as easy as it is delicious.

For the pastry:

150 g (5½ oz) lightly salted butter, very cold

250 g (9 oz/1⅔ cups) plain (all-purpose) flour

2 tablespoons demerara sugar

1 egg, beaten

For the sauce:

250 ml (9 fl oz/1 cup) thin (pouring/whipping) cream

1 star anise

1 thumb-sized piece of fresh ginger

4 cloves

2 cinnamon sticks

1 pinch grated nutmeg

250 g (9 oz) caster (superfine) sugar

1 tablespoon apple liqueur or Calvados

125 ml (4 fl oz/½ cup) apple juice

For the filling:

6–8 large tart cooking apples

3 tablespoons demerara sugar

50 g (1¾ oz) unsalted butter

1 egg, beaten

MAKE THE PASTRY. Work the diced butter, flour and demerara sugar together in a mixing bowl with an electric beater until the mixture is sandy. Add the beaten egg, mix again, then shape the dough into a ball with your hands. Wrap the dough in plastic wrap and place it in the fridge for at least 1 hour. Take it out 15 minutes before you use it.

MEANWHILE, MAKE THE SAUCE. Place the cream with the spices in a saucepan and bring to the boil. Take off the heat and let it infuse for at least 15 minutes. Strain the cream to remove the spices and set aside.

COMBINE THE SUGAR AND 100 ML (3½ FL OZ) OF WATER IN A HEAVY-BASED SAUCEPAN AND HEAT. Once the sugar has dissolved, bring to the boil and let the syrup bubble until it caramelises. Take off the heat and pour the hot spiced cream into the caramel (be careful of spatter!), stirring with a wooden spoon. Once the sauce is nice and smooth, add the apple liqueur or Calvados and apple juice. Set aside.

PREHEAT THE OVEN TO 180°C (350°F/GAS 4). Peel and dice the apples. Roll out the pastry into a circle. Place it on a baking tray lined with baking paper or a silicone mat.

SPREAD THE DICED APPLE OVER THE DOUGH. Sprinkle the pie with demerara sugar and pieces of butter. Fold over the edges of the pastry. Brush the edges with beaten egg and bake for about 30 minutes, until the pie is golden and the apples are very tender.

TAKE THE PIE OUT OF THE OVEN AND SERVE IT HOT OR JUST WARM WITH THE CARAMEL SAUCE. If you like you can accompany it with vanilla ice cream or crème fraîche.

STRAWBERRY, WATERMELON AND LEMONGRASS SOUP ×
with whipped cream

SERVES 6 / 15 MINS PREPARATION TIME

A very simple little soup, but one that everyone enjoys! Make it at the height of summer with beautiful seasonal fruit.

200 ml (7 fl oz) thin (pouring/ whipping) cream, well chilled
1 tablespoon icing (confectioners') sugar
700 g (1 lb 9 oz/4⅔ cups) ripe, juicy strawberries (make sure they're not tart!)

200 g (7 oz) watermelon
2 stems lemongrass

WHIP THE CREAM WITH AN ELECTRIC BEATER UNTIL VERY LIGHT, THEN ADD THE ICING SUGAR AND MIX IN WELL.

WASH, THEN HULL THE STRAWBERRIES. Remove the rind and cut the watermelon into cubes. Peel the lemongrass and cut it into sections. Put everything into the bowl of a blender and blend until you have a smooth purée.

STRAIN THE PURÉE TO REMOVE THE PIECES OF LEMONGRASS AND WATERMELON SEEDS.

POUR THE SOUP INTO GLASSES OR SMALL DESSERT BOWLS AND SERVE WITH THE WHIPPED CREAM.

✕ ALMOST NO-BAKE ✕
chestnut, apple and coffee cake

SERVES 8-10 / 40 MINS PREPARATION TIME / 10 MINS COOKING TIME / 2 HRS REFRIGERATION TIME

No baking (almost!) and not too sweet, this cake has everything going for it! Make sure you find the most chocolatey biscuits you can. Otherwise, add some cocoa powder with the butter at the beginning of the recipe.

5 tart cooking apples

About 600 g (1 lb 5 oz) chocolate biscuits

120 g (4¼ oz) lightly salted butter, melted

300 ml (10½ fl oz) thin (pouring/whipping) cream, well chilled

2 tablespoons mascarpone cheese

100 ml (3½ fl oz) very strong coffee

1-2 tablespoons icing (confectioners') sugar

5-6 tablespoons vanilla chestnut spread (crème de marrons)

PEEL THE APPLES, CUT THEM INTO SEGMENTS AND REMOVE THE SEEDS. Put them in a saucepan with a very small amount of water and cook over a medium heat for 10 minutes.

ONCE THE APPLES ARE NICE AND SOFT, PURÉE THEM UNTIL SMOOTH IN A BLENDER, THEN LET THEM COOL.

CRUSH THE BISCUITS AND COMBINE THEM WITH THE BUTTER. Line the bottom of a spring-form cake tin with this mixture. Press down well, then place the tin in the fridge for 2 hours to harden the base.

WHIP THE CREAM AND MASCARPONE WITH AN ELECTRIC BEATER UNTIL LIGHT, THEN MIX IN THE COFFEE AND ICING SUGAR.

SPREAD THE CHESTNUT SPREAD OVER THE BISCUIT BASE, THEN ADD A LAYER OF APPLE PURÉE ON TOP. Top off with the coffee-flavoured whipped cream and serve.

× RASPBERRY ROULADE ×

SERVES 6-8 / 15 MINS PREPARATION TIME / 20 MINS COOKING TIME / 2 HRS RESTING TIME

This dessert requires some delicate handling, but if it cracks a little, never mind, that's also very pretty!

4 egg whites
225 g (8 oz) caster (superfine) sugar
60 g (2¼ oz) flaked almonds
350 ml whipping cream, well chilled
2 tablespoons mascarpone cheese
2 tablespoons lemon curd (see recipe page 195)
200 g (7 oz) fresh raspberries

PREHEAT THE OVEN TO 200°C (400°F/GAS 6). Line a baking tray with baking paper or a silicone mat.

BEAT THE EGG WHITES TO SOFT PEAKS IN A MIXING BOWL WITH AN ELECTRIC BEATER, THEN ADD THE SUGAR IN THREE LOTS, BEATING WELL BETWEEN EACH ADDITION. The sugar needs to be completely dissolved.

ONCE THE MERINGUE IS GLOSSY AND FIRM, SPREAD IT OUT IN A RECTANGLE SHAPE ON THE BAKING TRAY. Scatter with the almonds, then bake for 15-20 minutes, until it is firm and golden on top.

TAKE THE MERINGUE OUT OF THE OVEN AND TURN IT OVER IMMEDIATELY ONTO A CLEAN TEA TOWEL (TEA TOWEL). Let it rest for about 10 minutes before removing the baking paper or silicone mat, then let it cool completely. Allow about 1 hour for this.

USING AN ELECTRIC BEATER, WHIP THE CREAM WITH THE MASCARPONE UNTIL LIGHT.

ONCE THE MERINGUE IS COMPLETELY COLD, SPREAD THE LEMON CURD OVER ONE HALF, LEAVING A BORDER OF 1.5 CM (⅝ INCHES). Cover with whipped cream, then scatter over the raspberries. Gently roll up the meringue on itself, without pressing too hard, then let it rest for 1 hour in the fridge before serving.

× LEMON AND BLUEBERRY TRIFLE ×
for ultra lazy dessert-lovers

SERVES 8-10 / 10 MINS PREPARATION TIME / 1 HR REFRIGERATION TIME

This trifle recipe is extremely simple, because all you need to do is layer the ingredients in a large and pretty clear dessert dish.

1 store-bought pure butter pound cake
100 ml (3½ fl oz) crème de cassis (blackcurrant liqueur)
350 ml (12 fl oz) thin (pouring/whipping) cream, well chilled
2 tablespoons mascarpone cheese
1 small jar blueberry jam
500 g (1 lb 2 oz) fresh blueberries
1 lemon, to decorate

For the lemon curd:

Zest and juice of 4 lemons
200 g (7 oz) caster (superfine) sugar
100 g (3½ oz) unsalted butter
3 whole eggs and 1 yolk

CUT THE POUND CAKE INTO SLICES AND MOISTEN WITH THE CRÈME DE CASSIS. Whip the cream and mascarpone together in a bowl with an electric beater until light.

MAKE THE LEMON CURD. Place the lemon zest and juice, sugar and diced butter in a bowl. Place this bowl over a saucepan of gently simmering water. Heat this mixture until the butter has melted, stirring from time to time and making sure the bottom of the bowl doesn't touch the water.

LIGHTLY BEAT THE EGGS AND THE EGG YOLK TOGETHER AND POUR THEM OVER THE BUTTER AND SUGAR MIXTURE. Cook, stirring gently and regularly, until the curd thickens and coats the back of a wooden spoon.

COOL THE CURD, STIRRING FROM TIME TO TIME. Cover with plastic wrap to stop a skin forming on the surface.

ASSEMBLE THE TRIFLES BY ALTERNATING SLICES OF LIQUEUR-MOISTENED POUND CAKE, LEMON CURD, BLUEBERRY JAM AND FRESH BLUEBERRIES. Top it all off with whipped cream.

LET THE TRIFLES REST IN THE FRIDGE FOR AT LEAST 1 HOUR. Decorate them with threads of lemon peel before serving.

✕ FRESH STRAWBERRY CARPACCIO ✕
with aromatic herb sugar

SERVES 4 / 10 MINS PREPARATION TIME

A great classic at my place: pretty, light and super easy to make. Don't deny yourself!

300 g (10½ oz/2 cups) strawberries, not too ripe

4 tablespoons caster (superfine) sugar

A few basil, mint or coriander (cilantro) leaves (or a combination of the three)

1 piece of zest from 1 lime

WASH THE STRAWBERRIES, HULL THEM AND SLICE THEM THINLY. Arrange them on plates in the style of a carpaccio.

PUT THE REST OF THE INGREDIENTS IN A BLENDER AND BLEND TO A GREEN POWDER.

ABOUT 10 MINUTES BEFORE SERVING, SPRINKLE THE STRAWBERRIES WITH THE GREEN SUGAR AND LET IT MELT ON TOP OF THE STRAWBERRIES. The sugar will mingle with the strawberry juices and create a delicious blend. Scatter with fresh herbs if you like. Serve.

✕ LEMON, BUTTERMILK AND DEMERARA SUGAR SCONES ✕
with crunchy lemon butter

MAKES ABOUT 8 SCONES / 10 MINS PREPARATION TIME / 12 MINS COOKING TIME

The buttermilk gives lightness to the scones, while the crunchy butter gives them zing ...

For the scones:

225 g (8 oz/1½ cups) plain (all-purpose) flour
75 g (2½ oz) lightly salted butter
1 tablespoon demerara sugar
1 egg
3 tablespoons buttermilk
Grated zest and juice of ½ lemon

For the butter:

150 g (5½ oz) lightly salted butter
2 tablespoons caster (superfine) sugar
Grated zest and juice of ½ lemon

MAKE THE SCONES. Mix together the flour, butter and demerara sugar in a mixing bowl with your fingers, until they have a texture similar to breadcrumbs.

IN ANOTHER BOWL, BEAT THE EGG WITH THE BUTTERMILK, THEN ADD THE LEMON ZEST AND JUICE. Mix this mixture into the previous one with a knife. Once the dough starts to come together, finish kneading by working it together again with your fingers. The dough should be pliable but not sticky. If it seems too dry, add a little buttermilk.

PLACE THE DOUGH ON A LIGHTLY FLOURED COLD SURFACE AND ROLL IT OUT WITH A ROLLING PIN TO A THICKNESS OF 2.5 CM (1 INCH), NO THINNER! Using a cookie cutter, cut out 8 rounds in the dough and place them on a baking tray lined with baking paper or on a silicone mat.

BRUSH THE SCONES WITH A LITTLE BUTTERMILK AND BAKE THEM FOR 10–12 MINUTES, UNTIL THEY ARE WELL RISEN AND GOLDEN.

MAKE THE LEMON BUTTER BY BLENDING TOGETHER THE BUTTER, CASTER SUGAR, ZEST AND LEMON JUICE IN A BLENDER UNTIL SMOOTH AND FLUFFY. Serve the butter immediately with the hot or warm scones.

✕ PANNA COTTA ✕
with coconut and lime

SERVES 6 / 20 MINS PREPARATION TIME / 3 HRS REFRIGERATION TIME

A dash of coconut and this panna cotta will be even more silky!

....

4 sheets gelatine

250 ml (9 fl oz/1 cup) thin (pouring/whipping) cream

250 ml (9 fl oz/1 cup) coconut milk

Grated zest of 1 lime

100 g (3½ oz) caster (superfine) sugar

....

SOAK THE SHEETS OF GELATINE FOR 5 MINUTES IN A BOWL OF COLD WATER TO SOFTEN THEM.

MEANWHILE, HEAT THE CREAM WITH THE COCONUT MILK IN A SAUCEPAN ON MEDIUM HEAT, WITHOUT LETTING THEM BOIL! Take off the heat, then add the lime zest and sugar. Stir well.

NEXT, SQUEEZE OUT ANY EXCESS WATER FROM THE SHEETS OF GELATINE AND ADD THEM TO THE HOT CREAM. Stir to dissolve the gelatine, then let the cream cool before pouring it into ramekins or glasses.

PLACE THE PANNA COTTAS IN THE FRIDGE FOR AT LEAST 3 HOURS (IDEALLY OVERNIGHT) SO THE CREAM IS COMPLETELY SET.

TO UNMOULD THE PANNA COTTA, WARM THE BOTTOM OF THE RAMEKINS OR GLASSES VERY GENTLY, THEN TURN THEM OVER ONTO THE SERVING PLATE. You can skip this step by setting the cream directly in small serving bowls or glasses.

$\times$ GRAPEFRUIT CURD $\times$

MAKES 400 G (14 OZ) CURD / 5 MINS PREPARATION TIME /
10 MINS COOKING TIME / 2 HRS REFRIGERATION TIME

A change from the lemon version! This recipe will surprise you with its slight bitterness ...

Juice of 2 pink grapefruit
(about 250 ml/9 fl oz/1 cup)
3 tablespoons grated
grapefruit zest

4 whole eggs and 3 yolks
70 g (2½ oz) unsalted butter,
diced

BRING THE GRAPEFRUIT JUICE TO THE BOIL IN A SAUCEPAN AND LET IT SIMMER FOR 5 MINUTES TO REDUCE BY HALF. Let it cool.

COMBINE THE GRAPEFRUIT JUICE AND ZEST WITH THE EGGS AND EGG YOLKS IN A SMALL MIXING BOWL. Place this bowl over a saucepan of gently simmering water and whisk the mixture for 8–10 minutes, until it thickens.

TAKE THE MIXING BOWL OFF THE HEAT AND MIX IN THE DICED BUTTER. At this stage, you can either strain the curd to remove the pieces of zest, or leave it a little 'rustic' if you prefer. Let the curd cool before placing it in the fridge for at least 2 hours.

206

· ICY ·

Glacé

241

✕ BANANA, MANGO AND DATE ✕
tarte tatin with crème fraîche ice cream

SERVES 6 / 10 MINS PREPARATION TIME /
25 MINS COOKING TIME / 1 HR CHURNING TIME

A sweet winter dessert lifted by the hint of tartness in the ice cream.

4 well-ripened bananas	1 ready-to-use sheet of
75 g (2½ oz) lightly salted	puff pastry
butter	**For the ice cream:**
150 g (5½ oz) caster (superfine)	500 g (1 lb 2 oz) crème fraîche
sugar	100 g (3½ oz) caster
3 soft fresh dates (Medjool if	(superfine) sugar
possible)	**Special equipment:**
3 pieces of soft dried mango	Ice cream maker

PREHEAT THE OVEN TO 180°C (350°F/GAS 4). Peel the bananas. Melt the butter with the sugar in a high-sided round cake tin or a cast-iron ovenproof frying pan. Let it caramelise for 1 minute, then add the bananas to brown in the caramel.

CUT THE DATES IN TWO, REMOVE THE PIT, THEN ADD THEM TO THE BANANAS IN THE FRYING PAN. Add the pieces of dried mango at the same time.

PLACE THE PUFF PASTRY DOUGH ON TOP OF THE FRUIT, TUCKING THE EDGES INTO THE SIDE OF THE PAN. Bake for 25 minutes, until the pastry is well puffed up and golden.

MEANWHILE, MIX THE CRÈME FRAÎCHE WITH THE SUGAR. Pour this mixture into the bowl of the ice cream maker and start the churn cycle.

TAKE THE TART OUT OF THE OVEN AND LET IT COOL FOR A FEW MINUTES (BUT NO LONGER). Turn it out onto a deep plate so it catches the caramel. Serve it with the just-set ice cream.

× ICE CREAM PIE WITH OATMEAL COOKIES ×
and butterscotch sauce

SERVES 8-10 / 25 MINS PREPARATION TIME /
1 HR REFRIGERATION TIME / 1 HR RESTING TIME

In cooking, and especially when making sweet dishes, there's no need to know all the cheffy techniques: assembling ready-made ingredients is your best friend. For this recipe, you can vary the ice cream flavours, but stay within the flavour range of caramel, chocolate, vanilla, almond, praline, etc.

For the ice cream pie:

About 400 g (14 oz) oatmeal cookies (with chocolate chips if you like), store-bought or home-made (see recipe page 56)
150 g (5½ oz) unsalted butter
2 litres (70 fl oz/8 cups) store-bought ice cream in your choice of flavour (vanilla, praline, etc.)

For the butterscotch sauce:

3 tablespoons caster (superfine) sugar
50 g (1¾ oz) lightly salted butter
100 ml (3½ fl oz) thin (pouring/whipping) cream

MAKE THE ICE CREAM PIE. Crush the cookies into crumbs. Melt the butter and combine it with the cookie crumbs.

LINE THE BOTTOM OF A TART TIN WITH THE RESULTING CRUMBLY MIXTURE. Let it harden in the fridge for about 1 hour.

CREATE A LAYER OF ICE CREAM ON TOP OF THE PIE BASE, EITHER BY SCOOPING IT OUT, OR SPREADING IT WITH A SPATULA.

MAKE THE SAUCE. Heat the sugar in a saucepan. Once the sugar starts to caramelise, add the butter and cream, heated beforehand. Stir well.

LET THE SAUCE COOL COMPLETELY (ALLOW ABOUT 1 HOUR), THEN POUR A LITTLE OVER THE PIE TO DECORATE BEFORE SERVING.

× VANILLA-SAUTÉED PINEAPPLE ×
with lime and coriander ice cream

SERVES 6 / 1 HR PREPARATION TIME / 1 HR CHURNING TIME / 10 MINS COOKING TIME

A little aromatic touch to highlight the tropical character of the pineapple.

For the sorbet:

225 g (8 oz) caster (superfine)
sugar plus 1 tablespoon
1 tablespoon grated zest from
1 lime
About 2 tablespoons fresh
coriander (cilantro) leaves
250 ml (9 fl oz/1 cup) freshly
squeezed lime juice

For the pineapple:

1 pineapple, not too ripe
1 large vanilla bean
50 g (1¾ oz) lightly salted butter

Special equipment:

Ice cream maker

MAKE THE SORBET. Combine 225 g (8 oz) of the caster sugar, the lime zest and 250 ml (9 fl oz/1 cup) of water in a saucepan. Bring to the boil, then let the syrup rest at room temperature.

FINELY CHOP THE CORIANDER LEAVES, THEN CRUSH THEM WITH THE TABLESPOON OF SUGAR. Add them to the previous mixture with the lime juice, then transfer everything to the ice cream maker before starting the churn cycle.

PREPARE THE PINEAPPLE. Peel the pineapple and cut it into very thin slices. Remove the tough, fibrous core if needed. Split the vanilla bean lengthways and scrape the seeds out with the point of a knife.

HEAT THE BUTTER IN A FRYING PAN (CAST IRON IF POSSIBLE). Add the slices of pineapple, the split vanilla bean and the vanilla seeds. Let the pineapple brown gently, basting it with its juices mixed with the butter and vanilla seeds.

ONCE THE PINEAPPLE IS SOFT AND A LITTLE CARAMELISED AROUND THE EDGES, TAKE IT OUT OF THE FRYING PAN AND SERVE WITH THE SORBET AND A LITTLE OF ITS COOKING JUICES.

⨯ GRILLED BANANA SPLIT ⨯
with dark rum caramel sauce and chocolate fudge sauce

A recipe inspired by the peerless American chef Emeril Lagasse, with the twist of TWO sauces for the price of one. You can of course make life easier for yourself and not grill the bananas ...

4 fairly firm bananas
6 tablespoons honey
6 tablespoons demerara sugar
4 scoops vanilla ice cream
3 tablespoons dry-roasted peanuts
Maraschino cherries

For the chocolate fudge sauce:

200 ml (7 fl oz) thin (pouring/whipping) cream
1 teaspoon instant coffee granules, dissolved in 1 tablespoon hot water (optional)
150 g (5½ oz) dark chocolate, roughly chopped

For the dark rum caramel sauce:

200 g (7 oz) caster (superfine) sugar
250 ml (9 fl oz/1 cup) thin (pouring/whipping) cream
80 g (2¾ oz) lightly salted butter
2 tablespoons black (dark brown) rum

For the whipped cream:

200 ml (7 fl oz) thin (pouring/whipping) cream, well chilled
2 tablespoons mascarpone cheese

MAKE THE CHOCOLATE FUDGE SAUCE. Heat the cream with the coffee in a saucepan, then pour it over the chocolate in a mixing bowl. Let it melt for a few minutes before stirring. Set aside. (You can keep this sauce in the fridge and reheat it gently before serving.)

MAKE THE DARK RUM CARAMEL SAUCE. Make a caramel by heating the sugar and 200 ml (7 fl oz) of water in a saucepan. Heat the cream in another saucepan. Once the caramel is golden brown, add the cream (be careful of spatter!), then add the butter and stir. If there are still lumps, return the sauce to the stove and heat gently. Finally, add the rum and set aside.

MAKE THE WHIPPED CREAM. Using an electric beater, whip the cream with the mascarpone until light.

PREHEAT THE OVEN GRILL (BROILER). Cut the bananas in two, lengthways, including the skin, and place them on a baking tray lined with baking paper. Pour over the honey and sprinkle with demerara sugar. Place them under the grill for 3–5 minutes, until the sugar caramelises. The bananas should still keep their shape as much as possible. Take them out from under the grill and remove their skin. Divide them between four plates (allowing two half bananas per guest) and add 1 scoop of vanilla ice cream.

SERVE THE BANANAS WITH THE SAUCES, THEN SCATTER WITH PEANUTS AND TOP WITH WHIPPED CREAM. Add a few cherries for a kitsch garnish.

✕ LEMON ICEBOX CAKE ✕

SERVES 6 / 30 MINS PREPARATION TIME /
1 HR CHURNING TIME / 5 MINS COOKING TIME

*A recipe inspired by a dessert served at
Lockhart restaurant in London.*

For the ice cream:

400 ml (14 fl oz) thin (pouring/
whipping) cream, well chilled
300-400 g (10½-14 oz) lemon
curd, store-bought or home-
made (see recipe page 195)
Juice and grated zest of
1 lemon

For the meringue:

2 egg whites

80 g (2¾ oz) caster (superfine)
sugar

For the base:

6 digestive biscuits (sweet
wholemeal biscuits)
30 g (1 oz) unsalted butter,
melted

Special equipment:

Ice cream maker

MAKE THE ICE CREAM. Using an electric beater, whip the cream in a mixing bowl until light, then mix in the lemon curd and the lemon juice and zest. Transfer everything to the bowl of the ice cream maker and start the churn cycle.

NEXT, MAKE THE MERINGUE. Beat the egg whites to soft peaks in a mixing bowl with an electric beater, then gradually add the caster sugar. Beat for another 3-4 minutes until the meringue is quite firm and glossy.

CRUSH THE BISCUITS AND COMBINE THEM WITH THE MELTED BUTTER. Divide this base between the bottom of six bowls or ramekins. Add 1 scoop of ice cream to each dish and cover with meringue. Place everything under a very hot oven grill (broiler) for a few moments or caramelise the meringue using a blowtorch. Serve straight away!

TWISTED BUTTER BISCUITS
with honey and orange flower frozen yoghurt

A recipe with Greek origins, perfect with summer fruit salads and orange salads in winter.

For the biscuits:

225 g (8 oz) unsalted butter, softened
150 g (5½ oz) caster (superfine) sugar
2 eggs
½ teaspoon natural vanilla extract
½ teaspoon bitter almond extract
275 g (9¾ oz/9¾ oz) plain (all-purpose) flour
peeled orange segments, to serve (optional)
chopped pistachio nuts, to serve (optional)

For the ice cream:

200 ml (7 fl oz) thin (pouring/whipping) cream, well chilled
500 g (1 lb 2 oz) plain yoghurt
5 tablespoons honey
½ teaspoon orange flower water

Special equipment:

Ice cream maker

PREHEAT THE OVEN TO 200°C (400°F/GAS 6). Line two baking trays with baking paper or silicone mats.

BEAT THE BUTTER WITH THE SUGAR IN A MIXING BOWL UNTIL PALE AND FLUFFY. Add 1 egg and keep beating. Add the vanilla and almond extracts, then the flour. Beat until you have a pliable dough.

SHAPE TEASPOONFULS OF DOUGH INTO SMALL SAUSAGES, THEN INTO 'S' SHAPES, BRAIDS OR EVEN SPIRALS.

PLACE THE BISCUITS ON THE TRAYS WITH A 3 CM (1¼ INCH) GAP BETWEEN THEM. Beat the remaining egg and brush it over the biscuits, then bake for 10 minutes, until the biscuits are firm and lightly golden. When they come out of the oven, let them cool on a rack.

MEANWHILE, MAKE THE ICE CREAM. Using an electric beater, whip the cream in a mixing bowl until light, then add the other ingredients, continuing to beat. Transfer the mixture to the bowl of the ice cream maker and start the churn cycle.

SERVE THE ICE CREAM WITH THE BISCUITS AND, IF YOU LIKE, SOME PEELED ORANGE SEGMENTS AND CHOPPED PISTACHIOS.

✕ MISO, COCONUT, ✕
maple syrup and ginger ice cream

SERVES 4-6 / 25 MINS PREPARATION TIME /
1 HR CHURNING TIME

This ice cream is stunning and excellent served with fresh tropical fruits.

400 ml (14 fl oz) coconut milk

150 g (5½ fl oz) maple syrup

1-2 tablespoons red miso paste
(Japanese soya bean paste,
from Asian food stores)

100 g (3½ oz) preserved
crystallised ginger

Special equipment:

Ice cream maker

PLACE THE COCONUT MILK, MAPLE SYRUP AND MISO PASTE IN A BLENDER. Blend until the mixture is very frothy.

TRANSFER THE MIXTURE TO THE BOWL OF THE ICE CREAM MAKER AND START THE CHURN CYCLE.

A FEW MINUTES BEFORE THE ICE CREAM IS COMPLETELY SET, ADD THE PIECES OF GINGER. Let the ice cream maker churn for a few seconds.

SERVE THE ICE CREAM IMMEDIATELY (ALWAYS BETTER!) OR KEEP IT IN THE FREEZER IF YOU WOULD LIKE TO ENJOY IT LATER.

$\times$ POPCORN ICE CREAM $\times$
with smoked chocolate sauce

SERVES 6 / 40 MINS PREPARATION TIME / 1 HR INFUSION TIME / 1 HR CHURNING TIME

This is my revamped version of an incredible dessert I had in London at the oh-so-hip Barnyard restaurant. You will find liquid smoke on the internet.

For the ice cream:

200 ml (7 fl oz) fresh full-cream (whole) milk

100 g (3½ oz) caramel popcorn

300 ml (10½ fl oz) thin (pouring/whipping) cream

4 egg yolks

100 g (3½ oz) caster (superfine) sugar

½ teaspoon natural vanilla extract

For the smoked chocolate sauce:

150 ml (5 fl oz) thin (pouring/whipping) cream, well chilled

200 g (7 oz) good quality milk chocolate, roughly chopped

1 tablespoon salted butter caramel (see recipe page 22).

A few drops of liquid smoke (a condiment with a smoky flavour for flavouring sauces or marinating meats, available on the internet)

Special equipment:

Ice cream maker

MAKE THE ICE CREAM. Bring the milk to the boil in a saucepan, then add the popcorn (set a little aside for decoration). Let it infuse for 1 hour.

STRAIN THE FLAVOURED MILK INTO A SAUCEPAN. Add the cream, stir and heat through.

MEANWHILE, BEAT THE EGG YOLKS WITH THE SUGAR IN A MIXING BOWL UNTIL PALE AND DOUBLED IN VOLUME. Pour the hot cream over this mixture and mix in, whisking vigorously. Return the mixture to the saucepan on the stove and stir with a wooden spoon until the custard thickens and coats the back of a spoon.

TAKE THE CUSTARD OFF THE HEAT AND POUR IT IMMEDIATELY INTO A LARGE MIXING BOWL TO STOP THE COOKING PROCESS. Add the vanilla extract. Let the custard cool before placing it in the fridge to cool down completely. Next, transfer it to the bowl of the ice cream maker and start the churn cycle.

MAKE THE CHOCOLATE SAUCE. Heat the cream in a saucepan, then pour it over the chocolate in a mixing bowl. Wait for 1 minute, then stir together well to melt the chocolate. Add the caramel and a few drops of liquid smoke. Stir well.

SERVE THE ICE CREAM WITH THE HOT SAUCE, GARNISHED WITH THE POPCORN.

CEREAL AND MILK
ice cream

**SERVES 6 / 40 MINS PREPARATION TIME /
1 HR CHURNING TIME**

A recipe that pays homage to Christina Tosi, the extraordinary pastry chef at Momofuku restaurant in New York.

75 g (2½ oz) caramelised puffed wheat breakfast cereal

350 ml (12 fl oz) fresh full-cream (whole) milk

2 tablespoons caster (superfine) sugar

Special equipment:

Ice cream maker

POUR THE CEREAL INTO A BOWL WITH THE MILK. Stir well and let the cereal soak up the milk (as if you were one of my teenagers who doesn't finish his breakfast and doesn't clear his plate away either!).

ADD THE SUGAR, THEN TRANSFER EVERYTHING TO THE BOWL OF THE ICE CREAM MAKER AND START THE CHURN CYCLE.

AS SOON AS THE ICE CREAM IS SET SERVE IT WITH SOME CRUNCHY CEREAL AND THE CHOCOLATE SAUCE FROM PAGE 221.

✕ NO-CHURN BROWN BREAD ✕
ice cream

SERVES 6 / 25 MINS PREPARATION TIME / 4 HRS FREEZING TIME

This ice cream is a great classic on gastro pub menus in Ireland and Great Britain. It is excellent with chocolate fudge sauce (see recipe page 213).

75 g (2½ oz) brown breadcrumbs

60 g (2¼ oz) light soft brown sugar

4 eggs

1 tablespoon whiskey

300 ml (10½ fl oz) thin (pouring/whipping) cream, well chilled

75 g (2½ oz) icing (confectioners') sugar

PREHEAT THE OVEN GRILL (BROILER) TO 200°C (400°F/GAS 6).

COMBINE THE BREADCRUMBS WITH THE SUGAR AND SPREAD ON A BAKING TRAY LINED WITH BAKING PAPER OR A SILICONE MAT. Place them under the oven grill for 5 minutes, until the crumbs are brown and caramelised, but make sure they don't burn! Remove from the oven and let them cool.

SEPARATE THE EGGS. Beat the egg whites to peaks in a mixing bowl with an electric beater.

IN ANOTHER MIXING BOWL, BEAT THE EGG YOLKS WITH THE WHISKEY. Gently fold this mixture into the beaten egg whites.

IN A THIRD CONTAINER, WHIP THE CREAM WITH THE ICING SUGAR USING AN ELECTRIC BEATER UNTIL LIGHT. Fold this into the previous mixture, then add the caramelised breadcrumbs.

TRANSFER EVERYTHING TO A LARGE PLASTIC AIRTIGHT CONTAINER AND PLACE IT IN THE FREEZER FOR AT LEAST 4 HOURS BEFORE SERVING.

$\times$ OLIVE OIL ICE CREAM $\times$

SERVES 4-6 / 15 MINS PREPARATION TIME / 20 MINS COOKING TIME /
4 HRS REFRIGERATION TIME / 1 HR CHURNING TIME

Too chic as a little summer dessert! Perfect with lemon and thyme biscuits.

200 ml (7 fl oz) fresh full-cream (whole) milk

100 ml (3½ fl oz) thin (pouring/whipping) cream, well chilled

140 g (5 oz/⅔ cup) caster (superfine) sugar

5 egg yolks

1 pinch fine sea salt

150 ml (5 fl oz) first cold pressed olive oil

Special equipment:

Ice cream maker

BRING THE MILK AND CREAM TO THE BOIL IN A SAUCEPAN.

WHISK THE SUGAR WITH THE EGG YOLKS IN A MIXING BOWL UNTIL THE MIXTURE IS PALE AND HAS DOUBLED IN VOLUME.

POUR THE HOT MILK OVER THE EGGS, WHISKING AT THE SAME TIME. Return everything to the saucepan and cook over a medium heat, stirring with a wooden spoon. Once the custard starts to thicken, remove it from the heat and let it cool before placing it in the fridge for a few hours.

MIX THE SEA SALT WITH THE OLIVE OIL AND POUR INTO THE CHILLED CUSTARD. Transfer everything to the bowl of the ice cream maker and start the churn cycle.

LEAVE THE ICE CREAM AT ROOM TEMPERATURE FOR A FEW MINUTES BEFORE SERVING.

✕ PEAR AND LYCHEE SORBET ✕
with saké

SERVES 4 / 30 MINS PREPARATION TIME / 1 HR CHURNING TIME

The little touch of saké gives a kick to this delicate sorbet.

....

3 pears
400 g (14 oz) tinned lychees in syrup
150 g (5½ oz) caster (superfine) sugar

150 ml (5 fl oz) saké

Special equipment:

Ice cream maker

....

PEEL AND DICE THE PEARS. Drain the lychees.

COMBINE THE SUGAR AND 300 ML (10½ FL OZ) OF WATER IN A SAUCEPAN. Add the pears and bring to the boil. Gently stew the pears for about 20 minutes before leaving them to cool completely.

DRAIN THE COOKED PEAR, THEN PURÉE IT IN A BLENDER, ADDING HALF THE LYCHEES AND THE SAKÉ. Adjust the consistency of the fruit purée by adding a little lychee syrup and/or pear poaching syrup.

TRANSFER THE MIXTURE TO THE BOWL OF THE ICE CREAM MAKER AND START THE CHURN CYCLE. Serve the sorbet with the rest of the lychees.

✕ BERGAMOT SORBET ✕

SERVES 4-6 / 30 MINS PREPARATION TIME /
1 HR REFRIGERATION TIME / 1 HR CHURNING TIME

If you can't find bergamot juice, just use fresh lemon juice instead.

100 g (3½ oz) caster
(superfine) sugar
400 ml (14 fl oz) bergamot
(bee balm) juice

Special equipment:

Ice cream maker

COMBINE THE CASTER SUGAR AND 150 ML (5 FL OZ) OF WATER IN A SAUCEPAN, THEN HEAT TO DISSOLVE THE SUGAR. Let the sugar syrup cool in the fridge for at least 1 hour.

COMBINE THE BERGAMOT JUICE WITH THE COLD SYRUP. Pour this mixture into the bowl of the ice cream maker and start the churn cycle.

LEAVE THE SORBET AT ROOM TEMPERATURE FOR A FEW MINUTES BEFORE SERVING.

× NEGRONI-STYLE ×
sorbet

SERVES 4 / 30 MINS PREPARATION TIME / 1 HR CHURNING TIME

A recipe inspired by Angela Hartnett, a great starred chef from a London restaurant.

150 g (5½ oz) caster (superfine) sugar
1 watermelon (to make about 400 ml/14 fl oz juice)
Juice of 5-6 oranges (about 250 ml/9 fl oz/1 cup)
Juice of 1 lemon
100 ml (3½ fl oz) red amaro liqueur (Campari)
50 ml (1½ fl oz) gin

Special equipment:

Ice cream maker

COMBINE THE SUGAR AND 125 ML (4 FL OZ/½ CUP) OF WATER IN A SAUCEPAN. Heat until the sugar has completely dissolved. Remove from the heat and set aside until the syrup cools, then place in the fridge to chill.

REMOVE THE WATERMELON RIND AND CUT UP THE FLESH. Remove as many seeds as possible, then purée the flesh in a blender. Strain the pulp to obtain the juice.

COMBINE THE COLD SYRUP WITH THE WATERMELON JUICE, ORANGE JUICE, LEMON JUICE AND THE ALCOHOLS. Transfer everything to the bowl of the ice cream maker and start the churn cycle.

LEAVE THE SORBET AT ROOM TEMPERATURE FOR A FEW MINUTES BEFORE SERVING.

× MINT AND LIME SORBET ×
with cumin-chilli chocolate bark

SERVES 6 / 30 MINS PREPARATION TIME / 1 HR CHURNING TIME

An ultra-light and very refreshing dessert, served with a thin chocolate tuile.

200 g (7 oz) caster (superfine) sugar
100 g (3½ oz) dark chocolate
½ teaspoon ground cumin
½ teaspoon ground chilli
1 small handful of fresh mint leaves
Grated zest and juice of 5 lemons
Grated zest and juice of 5 limes

Special equipment:

Ice cream maker

COMBINE THE SUGAR AND 275 ML (9½ FL OZ) OF WATER IN A SAUCEPAN AND BRING TO THE BOIL. Let the syrup simmer and reduce for 5 minutes.

MEANWHILE, MELT THE CHOCOLATE IN A MICROWAVE OR DOUBLE BOILER (SEE RECIPE PAGE 72). Spread it thinly over some baking paper and sprinkle very lightly with ground cumin and chilli. Keep the chocolate in the fridge until you serve the sorbet.

TAKE THE SYRUP OFF THE HEAT AND ADD THE MINT LEAVES. Let them infuse for about 5 minutes. Remove the mint leaves and let the syrup cool a little before adding the lemon and lime zests and juices. Combine well and place everything in the fridge until the syrup has completely cooled and chilled.

POUR THE SYRUP INTO THE BOWL OF THE ICE CREAM MAKER AND START THE CHURN CYCLE. Take the spiced chocolate bark out of the fridge, peel it off the baking paper and cut it into pieces as needed. Serve with the sorbet as soon as it has set.

× RASPBERRY AND RED CAPSICUM SORBET ×
with Sarawak pepper and fine sea salt chocolate crumbs

SERVES 6-8 / 45 MINS PREPARATION TIME / 1 HR CHURNING TIME / 4 HRS FREEZING TIME

Something different—a sorbet with a mixture of sweet and savoury flavours.

500 g (1 lb 2 oz) fresh raspberries
200 g (7 oz) peeled roasted capsicums (peppers) or piquillos (drained ones from a jar are perfect)
120 g (4¼ oz) caster (superfine) sugar
1 teaspoon raspberry vinegar
150 g (5½ oz) dark chocolate
6 dark chocolate biscuits
50 g (1¾ oz) unsalted butter
Sarawak peppercorns (available on the internet)
1 pinch fine sea salt

Special equipment:
Ice cream maker

PURÉE THE RASPBERRIES IN A BLENDER, THEN STRAIN THE PULP TO REMOVE THE SEEDS.

DO THE SAME WITH THE CAPSICUMS AND COMBINE THEM WITH THE RASPBERRIES, SUGAR AND VINEGAR.

TRANSFER THIS MIXTURE TO THE BOWL OF THE ICE CREAM MAKER AND START THE CHURN CYCLE. Place the sorbet in the freezer for 3-4 hours.

MELT THE CHOCOLATE IN A DOUBLE BOILER OR MICROWAVE (SEE RECIPE PAGE 72). Spread it into pretty shapes, very thin, on baking paper or a chocolate-making polypropylene sheet. Place in the fridge until serving time.

GRIND THE BISCUITS TO CRUMBS AND COMBINE THEM WITH THE BUTTER. Sprinkle with a pinch of freshly ground Sarawak pepper and a pinch of sea salt. Set aside in the fridge.

ASSEMBLE THE DESSERT ON THE PLATE WITH A SCOOP OF SORBET, THEN SOME BISCUIT CRUMBS AND CHOCOLATE SHAPES STUCK INTO THE SORBET. Serve immediately.

Let these granitas melt a little and drink them through a straw, like a smoothie.

Lychee Slushie

SERVES 2 / 15 MINS PREPARATION TIME / 4 HRS FREEZING TIME

400 g (14 oz) tinned lychees
in syrup
150 ml (5 fl oz) tinned coconut milk
Juice of 2 limes
4 tablespoons caster (superfine)
sugar
A few fresh lychees, to garnish

PURÉE ALL THE INGREDIENTS TOGETHER IN A BLENDER. Transfer everything to a plastic airtight container and place it in the freezer for about 4 hours, until the mixture is completely frozen.

TAKE THE CONTAINER OUT OF THE FREEZER, BREAK THE FROZEN MIXTURE INTO PIECES AND RETURN THEM TO THE BLENDER TO TURN THEM INTO SLUSH (THE CONSISTENCY OF MELTED SNOW). You can add sparkling water or lychee juice if you like.

GARNISH THE SLUSHIE WITH FRESH LYCHEES AND SERVE WITH STRAWS IN TALL GLASSES.

Watermelon Slushie

SERVES 2 / 15 MINS PREPARATION TIME / 4 HRS FREEZING TIME

½ watermelon
6-8 fresh mint leaves
4 tablespoons caster (superfine)
sugar
Juice of 3 limes
750 ml (26 fl oz/3 cups) sparkling
water

CUT UP THE WATERMELON FLESH AND PURÉE IN A BLENDER, PREFERABLY AFTER REMOVING AS MANY SEEDS AS POSSIBLE FIRST. Strain the watermelon pulp.

COMBINE THE WATERMELON JUICE WITH THE MINT AND SUGAR IN A BLENDER, THEN PURÉE. Transfer the mixture to a plastic airtight container and place it in the freezer for about 4 hours, until the mixture is completely frozen.

TAKE THE CONTAINER OUT OF THE FREEZER, BREAK THE FROZEN MIXTURE INTO PIECES AND RETURN THEM TO THE BLENDER TO TURN THEM INTO SLUSH (THE CONSISTENCY OF MELTED SNOW). Add the sparkling water and serve with straws in tall glasses.

× AFFOGATO ×

SERVES 6-8 / 3 MINS PREPARATION TIME

An incredibly effective dessert for a lunch with a chic edge. Serve the liqueur in a small glass beside the one containing the ice cream, then serve the espresso in a small pot on the side if you feel like playing the Pinterest stylist.

6-8 small scoops vanilla ice cream

3 espresso coffees

A little liqueur (amaretto, Tia Maria®, Kahlua, Baileys®, Grand Marnier®), whiskey, rum or Cognac

---

IF YOU THINK OF IT AHEAD OF TIME, MAKE SCOOPS OF ICE CREAM IN ADVANCE AND PLACE THEM ON A TRAY IN THE FREEZER.

MAKE THE COFFEES AT SERVING TIME SO THEY ARE HOT. Place 1 scoop of ice cream in the bottom of each glass or dessert bowl, then pour a little hot coffee over and a few drops of each guest's preferred alcohol or liqueur if you like.

· Recipe index ·

· Ingredient index ·

Coconut milk

Lychee slushie · 238

Miso, coconut, maple
syrup and ginger ice cream · 218

Pana cotta with coconut and lime · 200

Coffee

Affogato · 241

All home-made chocolate and
pear genoise, for the best bakers · 95

Almost no-bake chestnut, apple and
coffee cake · 191

Chocolate and coffee ice cream cake
with chocolate fudge sauce · 90

Chocolate café Liégeois · 21

Coffee and walnut cake
with buttercream icing · 139

Coffee, chocolate and hazelnut
dacquoise · 29

Grilled banana split with dark rum caramel
sauce and chocolate fudge sauce · 213

Irish coffee creams · 123

Mocha dacquoise · 86

No-bake fig, date and pecan traybake
with chocolate and coffee ganache · 89

Cognac

Affogato · 241

Lemon cake with Cognac · 168

Mocha dacquoise · 86

Oreo® cookie and cream cheese truffles
with mocha milkshake · 103

Vanilla rice pudding
with Armagnac prunes · 108

Cointreau

Christmas syllabub with cumquat
and cranberry compote · 111

Crêpes Suzette · 149

Cookies

CHOCOLATE COOKIES

Almost no-bake cake with
marrons glacés, apples and coffee · 191

Raspberry and red capsicum sorbet
with Sarawak pepper and fine sea salt
chocolate crumbs · 236

OATMEAL COOKIES

Ice cream pie with oatmeal cookies and
butterscotch sauce · 208

Coriander (cilantro)

Fresh strawberry carpaccio
with aromatic herb sugar · 196

Greek yoghurt with cinnamon, coriander,
brown sugar and chocolate · 115

Vanilla-sautéed pineapple
with lime and coriander ice cream · 211

Cranberries

Christmas syllabub with cumquat
and cranberry compote · 111

Cream cheese

Coffee and walnut cake with
buttercream icing · 139

Dark chocolate muffins with cream cheese
icing and caramelised peanuts · 96

Lemon cheesecake · 112

Oreo® cookie and cream cheese
truffles with mocha milkshake · 103

THE carrot cake · 133

The ultimate chocolate fudge cake
with cream cheese icing · 67

White chocolate cheesecake
with bourbon maple syrup · 107

Crème anglaise

L'Ami Jean's rice pudding with
caramel · 25

Crème de cassis

Lemon and blueberry trifle
for ultra lazy dessert-lovers · 195

Crème de marrons

Almost no-bake chestnut, apple
and coffee cake · 191

Mont blanc bites · 33

Croissants

Croissant pudding with caramel
and bourbon · 153

Cumin

Mint and lime sorbet with cumin-chilli
chocolate bark · 235

Cumquats

Christmas syllabub with
cumquat and cranberry compote · 111

Dates

Banana, mango and date tarte tatin
with crème fraîche ice cream · 207

Date, banana and honey cake with
whiskey icing · 144

No-bake fig, date and pecan traybake
with chocolate and coffee ganache · 89

Sticky date pudding · 135

Faisselle (soft curd) cheese

Fontainebleau · 44

Figs

No-bake fig, date and pecan traybake
with chocolate and coffee ganache · 89

Frangipane

Pear and almond tart · 40

Gin

Negroni-style sorbet · 232

Ginger

Pineapple tiramisu with ginger, yuzu and
whipped cream · 184

Chocolate cake with yuzu and
ginger icing · 75

Free-form apple pie with spiced
apple-caramel sauce · 187

Kiwifruit slushie · 239

Miso, coconut, maple
syrup and ginger ice cream · 218

Grand Marnier

Christmas syllabub with cumquat
and cranberry compote · 111

Crêpes Suzette · 149

Grapefruit

Grapefruit curd · 203

Guinness

Mint and lime sorbet with cumin and chilli
chocolate bark **235**

Watermelon slushie **238**

Meringue

Eton mess with rose, strawberry
and roasted rhubarb **177**

Miso

RED

Miso, coconut, maple
syrup and ginger ice cream **218**

Red miso buttercream **167**

WHITE

Shiro miso brownies **80**

Oatmeal

Oatmeal cookies **56**

Olive oil

Chocolate and almond olive oil cake **100**

Olive oil ice cream **226**

Orange marmalade

Marmalade and whiskey
bread and butter pudding **158**

Oranges

Chocolate and orange polenta cake **83**

Christmas syllabub with cumquat
and cranberry compote **111**

Clementine syrup cake **174**

Crêpes Suzette **149**

Eton mess with rose, strawberry
and roasted rhubarb **177**

Negroni-style sorbet **232**

Saffron crème brûlée with blood orange
sorbet and burnt butter biscuits **120**

Vanilla rice pudding
with Armagnac prunes **108**

Oreo® cookies

Chocolate, peanut butter
and Oreo® cookie tart **72**

Oreo® cookie and cream cheese truffles
with mocha milkshake **103**

Passionfruit

Passionfruit and mango pavlova **179**

Passionfruit panna cotta **124**

Peanuts

Dark chocolate muffins with cream cheese
icing and caramelised peanuts **96**

Grilled banana split with dark rum caramel
sauce and chocolate fudge sauce **213**

Peanut butter

Chocolate, peanut butter
and Oreo® cookie tart **72**

Peanut butter and jelly
bread and butter pudding **161**

Peanut butter cookies **55**

Pastry

PUFF PASTRY

Banana, mango and date tarte tatin
with crème fraîche ice cream **207**

Chocolate galette des rois with tonka bean
frangipane **92**

Tarte tatin with Calvados
crème fraîche **34**

SHORTCRUST PASTRY

Dark chocolate tart **37**

Peaches

Peach clafoutis with buttermilk sorbet
and rosemary sugar **183**

Pears

All home-made chocolate and pear
genoise, for the best bakers **95**

Brioche French toast à la Cyril Lignac **154**

Pear and almond tart **40**

Pear and lychee sorbet with saké **229**

Pecans

L'Ami Jean's rice pudding
with caramel **25**

No-bake fig, date and pecan traybake
with chocolate and coffee ganache **89**

Pineapple

Pineapple tiramisu with ginger, yuzu and
whipped cream **184**

Vanilla-sautéed pineapple

with lime and coriander ice cream **211**

Pine nuts

Pine nut, almond, lemon
and ricotta cake **142**

Pistachios

Clementine syrup cake **174**

Yoghurt cake with honey, rosewater
and pistachios **136**

Polenta

Chocolate and orange polenta cake **83**

Popcorn

Popcorn ice cream with smoked
chocolate sauce **221**

Pound cake

Lemon and blueberry trifle
for ultra lazy dessert-lovers **195**

Prunes

Vanilla rice pudding
with Armagnac prunes **108**

Raspberries

Pavlova **18**

Raspberry and red capsicum sorbet
with Sarawak pepper and fine sea salt
chocolate crumbs **236**

Raspberry roulade **192**

Raspberry or strawberry sorbet

Vacherin **30**

Rhubarb

Eton mess with rose, strawberry
and roasted rhubarb **177**

Rice

L'Ami Jean's rice pudding with caramel **25**

Vanilla rice pudding
with armagnac prunes **108**

Ricotta

Pine nut, almond, lemon
and ricotta cake **142**

Rosewater

Eton mess with rose, strawberry
and roasted rhubarb **177**

Published in 2016 by Murdoch Books, an imprint of Allen & Unwin
First published by Hachette Livre (Marabout) in 2014

Murdoch Books Australia
83 Alexander Street
Crows Nest NSW 2065
Phone: +61 (0) 2 8425 0100
Fax: +61 (0) 2 9906 2218
murdochbooks.com.au
info@murdochbooks.com.au

Murdoch Books UK
Erico House, 6th Floor
93-99 Upper Richmond Road
Putney, London SW15 2TG
Phone: +44 (0) 20 8785 5995
murdochbooks.co.uk
info@murdochbooks.co.uk

For Corporate Orders & Custom Publishing contact our business development team
at salesenquiries@murdochbooks.com.au.

Publisher: Corinne Roberts
Project Editor: Emma Hutchinson
Translator: Melissa McMahon
Design Manager: Megan Pigott
Art Director: Antoine Béon
Internal Graphic Designer: Pauline Ricco
Production Manager: Alexandra Gonzalez

A cataloguing-in-publication entry is available from the catalogue of the National
Library of Australia at nla.gov.au.

ISBN 978 1 74336 627 1 Australia
ISBN 978 1 74336 694 3 UK

A catalogue record for this book is available from the British Library.

Colour reproduction by Splitting Image Colour Studio Pty Ltd, Clayton, Victoria
Printed by 1010 Printing International Limited, China